D0036253

Living Thoughtfully,
DYING WELL

As a medical doctor in the U.S. and India for five decades, and as someone who almost died several times from heart illness, Glen Miller has done his homework on preparing to die. Living and dying are entwined. Miller's book rivets the reader's attention with his and others' stories. Readers will be torn between *not* wanting to stop and *needing* to stop because of the emotional and content depth. Preparing for death, in the ways Miller instructs us, will make our dying easier for loved ones who survive. This book is important for family and church discussion. Each chapter ends with discussion questions; it concludes with a checklist of tasks to set one's "house in order."
—**Willard Swartley**, *professor emeritus of New Testament at Anabaptist Mennonite Biblical Seminary*

Readable, realistic, and spiritually relevant, this book is for anyone coping with chronic illness or aging care issues, who yearns for the opportunity to die a "good death." Dr. Miller navigates the choppy waters of health care in ways that preserve personal dignity, maintain a sense of control, preserve moral and spiritual values, and generate loving and sustaining memories.
—**Clair Hochstetler**, *manager of chaplaincy and pastoral care at the Canberra Hospital, Australian Capital Territory*

In a world where the reality of death may be denied or resisted through futile and expensive effort, we need a book that provides a realistic and healthy perspective on this universal experience. Glen Miller has written that book. Using facts, figures, and especially stories, he addresses the legal, physical, and emotional aspects of dying to help us see death, and especially our preparation for it, in a positive way. This book is an inviting and useful guide to specific actions we can take to make our death what we want it to be.
—**Joseph Longacher**, *MD, past president of Mennonite Medical Association, and past president of medical staff at Henrico Doctors Hospital, Richmond, Virginia*

With good humor and frank honesty, experienced physician Dr. Glen E. Miller explores healthy living and dying in *Living Thoughtfully, Dying Well*. Poignant stories of others' end-of-life experiences accompany Dr. Miller's recounting of his own nearly fatal third heart attack. Readers will be challenged with the inevitable issues they must prepare for as they face the physical, emotional, and spiritual transitions of aging. This is a must-read for families and church communities.

—*Ruth Lapp Guengerich*, MEd, mental health counselor, codirector of Mennonite Women USA

Have you ever wished that you could talk with a family member about dying? Glen Miller provides reflective stories about his health journey, factual information about preparing for death, delightful humor, and thoughtful suggestions for conversation. Questions to guide discussions can be found at the end of every chapter. This book could facilitate conversations about choices and a good death by families or friends.

—*Mary J. Dyck*, associate professor at Mennonite College of Nursing, Illinois State University

As a member of a monastic community I appreciate so much Dr. Miller's expertise and approach to the issue of thinking ahead to one's death. In his Rule for Monasteries, Saint Benedict urges monastics to "keep death daily before one's eyes." As communities we are intentional about having members die "at home," surrounded by caring community members. This book is written in a warm, accessible manner, with stories and anecdotes bringing the major points into contact with the human situation. Each chapter concludes with questions that will draw the engaged reader into reflection and, hopefully, decision making and action. Miller argues in a convincing manner that it is possible and desirable to have a "good death" which truly integrates one's deepest human, spiritual beliefs.

—*Abbot John Klassen*, Order of Saint Benedict, Saint John's Abbey, Collegeville, Minnesota

Living Thoughtfully, DYING WELL

A Doctor Explains How to Make Death a Natural Part of Life

Glen E. Miller, MD

Herald Press

Harrisonburg, Virginia
Kitchener, Ontario

Library of Congress Cataloging-in-Publication Data
Miller, Glen E., 1932-
  Living thoughtfully, dying well : a doctor explains how to make death a
natural part of life / by Glen E. Miller.
    pages cm
  Includes index.
  ISBN 978-0-8361-9889-8 (pbk. : alk. paper) 1. Terminally ill—Care.
2. Terminally ill—Psychology. 3. Death—Psychological aspects. I. Title.
  R726.8.M55 2014
  362.17'5—dc23
                              2013043031

LIVING THOUGHTFULLY, DYING WELL
Copyright © 2014 by Herald Press, Harrisonburg, Virginia 22802
  Released simultaneously in Canada by Herald Press,
  Waterloo, Ontario N2L 6H7. All rights reserved.
Library of Congress Control Number: 2013043031
International Standard Book Number: 978-0-8361-9889-8
Printed in United States of America
Cover design: Merrill Miller; book design: Merrill Miller, Hannah Grieser
Cover photo: STILLFX/iStockphoto/Thinkstock

All rights reserved. This publication may not be reproduced, stored in a
retrieval system, or transmitted in whole or in part, in any form, by any
means, electronic, mechanical, photocopying, recording, or otherwise
without prior permission of the copyright owners.

Unless otherwise noted, Scripture text is quoted, with permission, from
the New International Version.

To order or request information, please call 1-800-245-7894 in the U.S.
or 1-800-631-6535 in Canada. Or visit www.heraldpress.com.

18 17 16 15 14   5 4 3 2 1

To Marilyn, for her decades of constancy and companionship; to Ken, Kori, Ed, and Janine and the wonderful people they married, Doris, Larry, Carolyn, and Dave, who continue to enlighten and stimulate me; and to my grandchildren who embody so much promise.

Contents

Foreword

THE WORDS *good* and *death* do not seem to fit together, but that's exactly what Dr. Miller urges his readers to seek: a good death. Unfortunately, most Americans will not plan for a good death, and many will suffer needlessly at the end of life. I've practiced in-hospital internal medicine for almost twenty-five years, and I see a steady stream of bad deaths.

I see elderly people suffer at the end of life and receive treatments I know they would decline if they could simply make informed decisions in advance. As I lecture and write about these issues, I regularly ask people how they would respond to this common scenario: You are elderly and have severe dementia (no short-term memory, unable to walk or feed yourself, bedfast and incontinent). You live in a nursing home. If you were to develop pneumonia, which might be fatal, which would you choose?

A. Transport me to the hospital for medical care to aggressively treat my pneumonia.

B. Keep me comfortable and treat my condition without transporting me to the hospital.

I think it's no surprise that most people choose option B. Unfortunately, in the United States about 93 percent of people with severe dementia in nursing homes will be transported to a hospital. This often includes intensive care unit treatment, and many times these patients become confused and must be physically restrained. Most people would not like to die this way: in a hospital, in an intensive care unit, on a breathing machine, and physically restrained.

The best way to avoid a bad death is to plan for a good death. This includes being able to be at peace with God, your family, and friends, and to leave this life without substantial regrets. It also means that you plan ahead with your family and physician so that you will receive only the types of medical care that you agree to in advance. Dr. Miller points out that 80 percent of people say they want to die at home, yet only 25 percent do so, and it is because they have not planned for the future.

One problem for elderly patients is that the vast majority are not able to make medical decisions when they are admitted to the hospital. Severe illnesses often affect cognitive function, and that's especially the case for the elderly. Under these circumstances, a family member is thrust into the role of decision maker. That's often a traumatic experience if the decision maker has not discussed the issues with the patient in advance. Sadly enough, according to a Pew Research Center poll (2006), fewer than 30 percent of people have designated a decision maker and discussed the issues; thus, most people have decision makers acting for them who are not aware of their desires in the face of the medical problems. The result is that these decision makers often opt for aggressive care ("Do everything!"), and about one-third of the decision makers suffer emotionally from this trauma. All of this is preventable with planning and discussion *in advance*.

You can plan for your future and how you want your life to end. That planning will ensure that you receive the type of medical care that fits your preferences, and that your loved ones will not be traumatized by making decisions for you without your input. When you face the reality of death and plan for it carefully, you will find that you are free to live life with vigor and joy.

Dr. Miller uses real-life examples to illustrate his points, including interviews and stories from individuals with a variety of backgrounds, making the topic widely applicable. The case study format makes this book engaging and applicable. I hope that many people will read this book thoroughly and complete the planning checklist. If you do, then you will reach Dr. Miller's goal: you will plan for a good death. It will benefit both you and your family.

—*Jeff Gordon, MD*

Preface and Acknowledgments

AN ELDERLY WOMAN wanted to talk to me after I finished my presentation on the escalating cost of healthcare. She had a story to tell—the story of how her husband had died. This was the first of many stories I heard on this theme. I caught the frustration of surviving family members in making end-of-life decisions with limited medical knowledge. For some there were persistent lingering questions and regrets about how the process of dying had gone. The enduring question was "Did we do right by our loved one at the end of life?" Elderly people and their families were searching for helpful ways to prepare for the inevitable final end—death.

*Did we do right by our loved one
at the end of life?*

The need to prepare for death took center stage for me personally after my cardiac arrest in September 2010. With a medical history of two previous heart attacks, bypass surgery, and a pacemaker, it was no longer plausible for me to ignore my significantly reduced life expectancy. Barring a fatal accident, I knew what to expect at the end of my life. And the end was in sight.

I determined to do whatever possible to make my time of passing a time of peace and serenity. Above all, I wanted to create memories for my family that would allow them to recall my passing—yes, with sadness—but without regret or remorse for the decisions made.

Loving relationships at the time of dying are an essential part of a good death. In a seven-year association with Mother Teresa, I witnessed Mother and her Missionaries of Charity fulfilling their mission to provide comfort to the poor and dying on the streets of Calcutta. Mother Teresa spoke eloquently about the transformation that love and human touch can make for a dying person picked up off the streets of Calcutta. That loving presence is no less important for each of us.

I have a number of advantages in writing about preparation for death: (1) As a physician, I cared for dying patients. (2) As a hospital administrator and author of a book on the subject, I understand the workings of the healthcare system. (3) As a patient, I experienced the need to make far-reaching and urgent medical decisions under the stress of uncertainty and time limitations. (4) With a degree in theology, I recognize dying as a *spiritual* event—more so than a physical, emotional, social, or psychological one. (5) I've also led seminars for seniors and their families on the subject.

Besides my own experiences, medical knowledge, and research into technological and ethical issues, my book draws on what I've learned from interviews with people approaching death. Usually these discussions started off on the theoretical, but invariably the conversation turned personal. Priests and pastors, monks, social workers, chaplains, adult children, believers, and agnostics—everyone—had their story that they needed to tell. I also interviewed clergy and individuals from diverse religious and philosophical backgrounds centered on how they bring comfort and hope to dying patients and their families.

This book was written in the hope and expectation that it will be useful primarily for elderly persons facing death with their families. It deals with the diminishment that comes with aging and chronic disease, the recognition of approaching death, and the preparation necessary for a good death.

The book does not address the death of a child or younger adult. In the last several years, the community where I live experienced the deaths—after prolonged struggles with cancer—of a seven-year-old child and a thirty-seven-year-old mother of three small boys. The latter was one of the pastors of the church I attend. The loss of children and people in the prime of life is excruciatingly painful. A quick survey of Amazon and other bookstores reveals many books written that address these losses. *Living Thoughtfully, Dying Well*, however, is written specifically for elderly or chronically ill persons and their families.

This book was written for both U.S. and Canadian readers. I recognize that there are radical differences between the healthcare systems in the United States and Canada. However, the need to actively prepare for a good death transcends the border between our two countries. Included in the book are a few comparisons between the two healthcare systems, such as advance directives and medical malpractice. There is a more detailed side-by-side comparison of the U.S. and Canadian healthcare systems in the appendix.

I am indebted to all those who willingly shared their personal stories of the times of laughter and pain, joy and sadness, quiet contentment or lasting regrets as a loved one died. I felt honored to be taken into the confidence of those who shared their deepest feelings.

I want to thank the other participants at the Collegeville Institute, particularly director Don Ottenhoff, Professor Michael McGregor, and author Kathleen Norris for their helpful guidance and encouragement. I am grateful to the persons who read the manuscript and made insightful and helpful suggestions: Father Kilian McDonnell, Dr. Douglas Smucker, Willard Swartley, Clare Schumm, Ruth Guengerich, Mary

Dyck, and Kathleen Rempel Boschman. I learned from the feedback of participants in Sunday school classes and workshops, which taught me how to best communicate concepts and issues. Edgar Metzler, with a small cadre of other people, faithfully fed me articles and other references that helped shape this book.

I particularly want to thank my wife, Marilyn. In fifty-seven years we have experienced so much together—long periods of relative deprivation as I got my training, the uncertainties of schedules and plans in dealing with my on-call times, and the eleven years we lived overseas when we were the main source of support for each other. Her insights, suggestions, and critique were invaluable in writing this book. She was patient as I disappeared for hours into my office only to emerge all too often preoccupied and absentminded.

Thanks to Amy Gingerich of MennoMedia for her early expression of interest in this book. Melodie Davis, my editor, also deserves special mention for her editing expertise, the suggestions on how to improve the manuscript, and for shepherding it through to publication.

Introduction

THE ADVANCES in medical technology over the past fifty years have been breathtaking, extending life expectancy nearly a decade and giving millions of people a better quality of life. No one would want to revert to the past. But the advances in medical technology and treatment have created a new set of problems, especially regarding end-of-life issues.

The way we die has changed.

The way we die has changed. Before the advent of cardiopulmonary resuscitation (CPR), magnetic resonance imaging (MRI), computerized axial tomography (CAT) scans, pacemakers, defibrillators, and automatic respirators, death was a relatively simple thing. Barring a life-ending accident, a person's health gradually declined due to aging or chronic disease. In 1965, most of what I could do for a patient was available in the doctor's bag I carried on house calls. There were relatively few options for diagnosis and treatment. With the advances in medical technology came the potential for many more diagnostic procedures and methods of treatment. Decisions must be made.

This need for decisions requires much more active participation from the patient and family than in years past.

The decisions made in the process of dying will determine the quality of the dying experience for the patient and family. Planning *where to die* is a critical part. There are times when death in an intensive care unit is unavoidable, but too many older people die there, connected to tubes and monitors and unable to communicate with their families. Visiting daughters and sons feels awkward, not knowing where to stand, let alone how to comfort their loved one. Ruth (chapter 4) was in exactly that situation, tethered to her bed with catheters and monitor wires. Her arms were tied to the side of the bed to keep her from pulling out the tubes vital to keeping her alive. Her last words to her family were "Untie me now!" They now live with the memory that their mother left this life agitated and out of touch with her close-knit family.

Preparation starts with an awareness of one's mortality.

Ruth's death stands in contrast to my sister's death. Although she was dying of a brain tumor at seventy-four, Lois was calm and at peace, lying in her bed at home, surrounded by family members expressing their love and appreciation for her. She died as simply as she had lived, trusting in a loving God and resting in the comfort of her supportive community.

I gained impetus to write this book from my personal desire to plan for *my* good death. This became urgent as I realized that I'm dying myself. We all are, of course, but my situation is more acute. I've survived two heart attacks and two incidents of cardiac arrest. I don't know how long I can expect to live, but with my cardiologist's diagnosis of congestive heart failure, my life expectancy is certainly reduced.

What I wish for myself, I wish for all: a good death that allows us to leave this world as naturally and positively as possible. The prospects of a good death are greatly enhanced if steps are taken to prepare for it.

The process of preparation starts with an awareness of one's mortality. It is so easy to put off thinking about death. Even though I had made desultory efforts to prepare for death earlier, it was my cardiac arrest that grabbed my attention. This led to a conversation with family members about my wishes for medical care in my time of dying. Since about 85 percent of us will not be able to speak for ourselves at the end of life, I identified someone who understands my desires and will speak for me if I am unable.

Preparation will increase the possibility that dignity and privacy will be respected in the time of dying. Preparation will give both patient and family a sense of control when events tend to spiral out of control. Most importantly for me, loving family memories can be created that will allow conversation about my passing without feelings of remorse.

Chapters 5 and 6 contain many practical suggestions— divesting of possessions, preparing a living will and advance directives, and making funeral plans and plans to die at home. Chapters 7 and 8 deal with death as a spiritual event and provide ways to give expression to beliefs and values that can be applied to decisions for end-of-life medical care.

I have included questions and suggestions for discussion after each chapter. The takeaway from this book will be greatly enhanced as you discuss these issues with your family, Sunday school class, or a group of friends.

Some of my recent conversations in preparing to write this book were with Father Kilian, a ninety-year-old Benedictine monk at St. John's Monastery in Minnesota. We were two old guys from vastly different backgrounds and religious communities—Catholic and Mennonite—talking candidly about faith and the process of dying. The conversation we had on dying is in chapter 2. At the end of our last time together, we each prayed a blessing for the other. Kilian said, "I've never had a conversation like this before." Neither had I.

Newspapers, radio, and television are replete with programs talking about the need to plan for making good end-of-life healthcare decisions. In a recent California survey, 60 percent of respondents said that they were concerned with this issue, yet 57 percent said they had done nothing about it.

A good death takes planning. I hope that this book will encourage elderly persons and their families to actively prepare for that good death. With good preparation in your time of dying, *you will be more likely to*

- maintain your dignity and privacy;

- have a sense of control over events;

- die in a way that reflects the way you lived;

- create loving memories for your family;

- reduce your costs; and

- die at home.

Everyone deserves a good death surrounded by loved ones in an atmosphere of peace and serenity. That's what I want for myself and that's what I hope for everyone.

One

The Wake-Up Call

In three words I can sum up everything I've learned about life: it goes on. —Robert Frost

CARDIAC ARREST!

The nurse yelled, "Someone call 911!" The keynote speaker of the evening had suddenly disappeared behind the podium, lying on the floor with a pool of blood collecting around his head. Mark, a battalion chief in the fire department, sprang into action. His training and experience had prepared him for situations exactly like this. He found no pulse and quickly confirmed that the speaker had collapsed because of a cardiac arrest. Kathy, a hospital-based nurse trained in CPR (cardio-pulmonary resuscitation) rushed to help. They cut off his blue blazer, shirt, and tie and began closed chest massage. Mark took charge with calm authority, calling on his years of training in CPR.

She later told me, "I thought you were dead."

I was the speaker. My wife, Marilyn, had been sitting on the speaker's dais with me. About five minutes into my speech, she saw me suddenly keel over backward. The only sound was when my head thumped on the step behind me. She later told me, "I thought you were dead."

Without any warning, my heart lost its effective rhythm and was no longer pumping blood throughout my body. The heart rhythm—ventricular fibrillation—left my heart a quivering mass, useless as a pump. The heart urgently needed an electric shock to convert back to a normal rhythm. Oxygen essential to my survival was no longer reaching my brain, heart, or other vital organs. Without oxygen, in a few minutes enzyme systems in cells would come to a halt and cells would begin to die by the millions or billions. After that, there can be no recovery.

Mark and Kathy started CPR, compressing my chest about 120 times a minute, squeezing blood from my now flabby heart to keep vital organs supplied with oxygen until the heart rhythm could be reestablished. Jeff, an anesthesiologist who was at the meeting only because his father catered the meal, also hurried to help. Mike, a county councilman with CPR training, took his turn at the exhausting work of the rapid-fire chest compressions.

The EMT (emergency medical technician) squad arrived seven minutes later. Their monitor recorded the chaotic beat of a struggling heart. Mark was greatly relieved to see that my heart converted to a functional rhythm after the first electric shock from the defibrillator. My heart was now beating in a coordinated way and responding to the pacemaker that had been pacing my heart for the past four years. I again had a pulse and blood flowing through my body from my beating heart.

Nancy, a local pastor, and Pat, a parish nurse, enfolded my wife in their arms as all this activity swirled about them. She watched as the squad loaded me into the ambulance. In the ambulance, Marilyn, who is a nurse, took comfort when she saw that I was breathing without assistance. She heard the squad members discuss where they were to take me and was greatly relieved to hear me say, "Take me home." They rightly ignored me.

My resuscitation was a community effort that included a firefighter-paramedic, nurse, doctor, county councilman, parish nurse, hospital chaplain, and two pastors, each doing their part with compassion and competence. And, as if to cover all the bases, a Pentecostal pastor had prayed for my welfare. That's community in action.

CONFUSION GRADUALLY CLEARS

I had been speaking to a group of about 120 people at the annual meeting of the St. Joseph Valley Project whose motto is "Jobs with Justice." I was on the third PowerPoint slide that graphically illustrated the escalating cost of healthcare. That much I remember.

The first two days in the hospital are essentially lost to me—only snippets of memory remain. Yet the brain has a remarkable capacity to adjust. I was told that throughout these first two days I engaged in lucid conversations and responded to questions appropriately. I kept asking what had happened even though I was answered each time. I compared my medical training with that of my cardiologist in detail and a few minutes later asked him about his training again.

During that time I recall that my pastor, Mary, came to visit. She said, "I know that in the past months you have been talking about how we pray in situations like this. So how do you want us to pray for you?" I remember thinking that this was an important question and I made a conscious effort to concentrate. I replied, "Two things: that I have patience with what needs to be done, and that I can continue to have meaningful relationships."

The worst time in the hospital was during the second night. I woke up with a sense that I needed to do something and got out of bed. I stood at the side of my bed and realized I had no idea where I was. I thought, "I have been in this situation before when traveling. I will be able to figure out where I am." But now, despite my best efforts and concentrating, I just couldn't get oriented. I was intensely frustrated. Suddenly, four nurses came hustling into the room. The smallest nurse came to me and got right up in my face and said, "Dr. Miller, you are in the hospital. You can't just get out of bed without help." This nurse seemed so agitated that I felt I needed to pacify her and patted her on the shoulder and assured her that I was all right.

I realized that I could have been permanently confused and disoriented.

I got back into bed and surveyed my room: I had a bed that understands five languages, a cardiac monitor dutifully showing each heartbeat, and a camera in the upper corner of the room. It dawned on me that the nurses had been watching me on the camera.

Then it hit me that I had been disoriented, unaware of where I was. I remembered other confused patients and how they tried to cover up their confusion. I felt I had embarrassed myself standing there at the bedside, disoriented, in my open-in-the-back hospital gown.

Later, after I had further recovered, a wave of gratefulness washed over me as I realized that I could have been permanently confused and disoriented with a brain that had lost its ability to remember. Each morning since then, as I get out of my bed, I am so grateful that I regained my mental faculties that allow me to feel and remember and interact with other people.

As I gradually regained my memory, I reflected on what was happening. I was interested in how my mind worked. On the third hospital day, I followed a long habit and asked for pen and paper to record my understanding of what was happening. I recorded notes that were chronological and insightful. After I arrived back home days later, I discovered two sets of nearly identical notes. I recalled the second set but had no recollection of the first.

Also on the third hospital day, I told our son Ken, a medical doctor, that I wanted to talk to the cardiologist about his reason for doing a heart catheterization. Even though I was not functioning on all cylinders yet, this concern came from my interest in using the healthcare system as efficiently as possible and avoiding unnecessary expense.

Later that day, Ken came into my room holding the get-well card from Mother Teresa that I had received in 1996 after my first heart attack.[1] He held the card up in front of me and said, "Dad, you are the patient here." Ken read the words of Mother Teresa to me, "'Be the little lamb in the arms of Jesus who loves you.' As Mother Teresa said, allow the doctors to do what they feel best." I agreed to the catheterization, which was done the next day.

Part of who I am is reflected in my sense of humor. When my sense of humor returned, Marilyn was convinced I was on my way to full recovery of my mental capacity. On the third hospital day, Marilyn was helping me order my next meal. She asked, "What would you say to baked fish?" I replied, "I would say 'Hello fish, how are you today? Was it uncomfortably warm where you were? Do you feel especially tender today?'" On my fourth hospital day I received a new pacemaker that is designed to shock the heart back into a normal rhythm if fibrillation recurs. I was assured that I could resume normal activity.

Having survived, I am left with a heightened sense of gratefulness for simple things: the love of family, just getting up in the morning to start a new day, and the prospect of continued

---

1. My first heart attack occurred in Calcutta. Among the get-well cards was one from Mother Teresa whom I had known over the previous five years. It was a postcard picture of Jesus carrying a lamb followed by sheep. On the lamb in Jesus' arms Mother Teresa had written the word "You." On the back side she wrote: "Dear Dr. Glen E. Miller, Be the little lamb in the arms of Jesus who loves you. I will pray for you [to] get well soon. God Bless You," M. Teresa, MC.

participation in the things that give life meaning. I have been given more time; I know not how many days, weeks, months, or years.

As a doctor, I had been there dozens of times. I felt the sickening snap of brittle ribs breaking while performing CPR on an octogenarian. I know the feeling of futility when there is no response by the injured heart and the sense of failure as we stop our resuscitation efforts. Even today, some of these failures stick in my mind, like the father who only wanted to live to see his twin sons play basketball on their high school team. The immensity of the tragedy for this family struck me like a physical blow.

A tragedy that never seems to end is when the patient survives physically but her brain is damaged due to a lack of oxygen for too long a period. The degree of injury is relative to the length of time the brain was oxygen deprived. In severe injury, the person never regains consciousness and is in a permanent vegetative state. Less severe damage can cause lasting confusion, stroke-like weakness, speech problems, or loss of short-term memory. In these situations, the surviving family may live with their loved one for years, present in body only, reminding them of what might have been.

THE THIRD TIME

The cardiac arrest on the speaker's podium was the third time my heart trouble showed itself. The first time, in 1996, I was living in Calcutta, India. We were at a tennis club for the weekend celebrating our fortieth wedding anniversary. Early on a Sunday morning, while playing tennis, I gradually became aware of an all-consuming tiredness. I asked for a time out and when the aching fatigue did not improve, I walked to my room nearby. On that short walk, my physician instincts kicked in and I realized that I was having a heart attack. Marilyn reached the local physician on call who turned out to be a pediatrician.

In order to ensure admission directly to a cardiac care unit, we rehearsed the classical symptoms of a heart attack—compressing chest pain radiating to the left arm, sweating, and extreme tiredness. Marilyn and the taxi driver walked me from the hotel room to the curbside taxi and twenty minutes later we were in the hospital. My description of the symptoms had convinced the pediatrician, and I was admitted directly into the cardiac intensive care unit, where a major heart attack was confirmed.

During the first night in the hospital, I had a vivid dream. The images of that dream stick with me to this day. I was in the hold of a large ship, all by myself. There was a red door near the front of the room where the ship came to a point. The door swung open and I saw water rushing forward, telling me that the ship was backing away from the pier. I decided that if I was going to get off the ship, I needed to jump. I jumped to the pier and the dream ended.

The next morning I learned that during the night my heart had slowed to about thirty-three beats a minute. I was given an injection and my heart rate increased. I have no way to prove that my dream was at the same time as the slowing of my heart. But it was clear to me that if I had been in the Indian village two weeks before, thirty-six hours away from any medical care, I would not have survived.

With this heart episode, I pondered the question of why I survived. One answer suggested that I had special favor in the sight of God. I rejected that concept. On the other hand, I felt that I had survived for a purpose, that there was need for me to continue to contribute to those around me. Thereafter, each day I got up with a mild feeling of urgency that I needed to get on with the rest of my life, whatever that turned out to be.

Ten years later, similar feelings returned. I had been under medical care for my coronary artery disease. I had a meeting one hundred miles from my home and didn't feel well and had difficulty mustering the energy to go. Marilyn drove me to the meeting. After returning home and a nap, I felt quite well. However, that evening before going to bed, I checked my blood pressure and found that my pulse was again thirty-three beats per minute.

In the hospital ER, the EKG (electrocardiogram) showed that I had experienced a small heart attack and blood tests indicated moderate heart muscle damage. I was admitted to the

It was now three times that fate or luck or a divine plan had allowed me to survive.

hospital. The next day a heart catheterization showed that the main coronary artery was 95 percent blocked. This artery is so important to supplying the heart with vital blood flow that when it closes, the patient almost always dies. For that reason, this artery has the nickname "the widow maker."

Several days later, I was placed on a heart/lung machine with my heart at standstill for about four hours. The blockages in four arteries were bypassed with vein grafts taken from my legs. The surgeon told Marilyn that sometimes they are unable to restart the heart in patients who had a previous heart attack. My widow maker artery *hadn't* closed and my heart restarted successfully. I had averted a major catastrophe and had again survived. That was the second time.

FATE, LUCK, OR DIVINE PLAN?

It was now three times that fate or luck or a divine plan had allowed me to survive against the odds. I felt a kinship with people who "miraculously" lived through a tsunami when others all around them did not, or with the person who survived cancer when another patient with a similar diagnosis did not.

On assessing this issue of why I survived when others didn't, my thoughts repeatedly turned to my good friend Mike. He is a gifted musician with the violin and drums and leads singing in our congregation. As a physician, Mike's patients explicitly trusted him to guide their medical care. He is known for a high level of competence and unfailing kindness and gentleness of spirit.

Mike's patients and our entire community were shocked when he announced his retirement at age fifty-nine. His plans for retirement had been formulated one year earlier when he noticed that his ability to remember details and work through complicated problems was not up to his usual standards. He recalled that other male members of his extended family had early-onset Alzheimer's disease. An evaluation by a neurologist confirmed the diagnosis. Mike confided in his medical colleagues and office staff and made plans for retirement that would provide ongoing care for his patients. His forced retirement and diminished prospects for the future are a tragic loss to his family, his church, and his community.

Mike is a good friend. The thought kept returning to me that if I, nineteen years older than Mike, could somehow trade life's fortunes with him, I would happily do it. But that's not a choice either Mike or I have.

THE LASTING THOUGHT

I learned several things from my cardiac arrest. I knew the long odds that I would survive a cardiac arrest, and the even more remote possibility that I would regain my mental faculties. As I thought about this, I visualized a virtual parade of

There are things worse than death.

patients I had cared for who had physically survived but were left with severe mental impairment—Marvin, who was transferred back to my care from an out-of-town cardiac arrest and now was in a persistent eyes-wide-open vigilant state, looking like he was just about to wake up but never would. Or octogenarian Maynard, who suffered multiple broken ribs in the resuscitation efforts and remained unconscious and on a ventilator for four days until he died. Less dramatic but no less tragic are the persons with gradual onset of dementia. I recall the daughter who faithfully recited the news to her silent and confused mother who comprehended nothing.

It was clear to me that there are things worse than death. I was determined to proactively prepare for my own time of dying.

QUESTIONS AND SUGGESTIONS FOR DISCUSSION

1. Who would you turn to if there is a sudden medical crisis?

2. What preparation have you made for a medical crisis?

3. Have you experienced a medical crisis or severe accident—your own or a friend's or relative's—that caused you to think that you will not live forever? Has the death of a friend or relative stirred this question in you? Share.

4. What does the phrase *mortality awareness* mean to you?

5. How can the church or a group of like-minded people help to keep in view the idea that life is precious and will have an end?

6. How does your faith inform you at the time of a crisis?

Two

Good Deaths and Bad Deaths

I took a man I picked up from the street to our Home for the Dying in Calcutta. When I was leaving he told me, "I have lived like an animal on the streets, but I am going to die like an angel. I will die smiling." He did die smiling, because he felt loved and surrounded by care.
—Mother Teresa

"**SO WERE YOU DEAD?**" The young news photographer had sidled up to me and asked his question in the hushed tone of a sacred place. It was six weeks after my cardiac arrest and we had just finished a press conference arranged to promote public CPR training. He had heard the story of my collapse without pulse or breathing. In his mind that meant I had died.

I explained to this puzzled man that by the old definition I was indeed dead—my heart had stopped and I was no longer breathing. I was a few minutes from being *irretrievably* dead. Without CPR I would have been dead—*permanently*—within five to seven minutes when my enzyme systems would have failed and my organs died. There is no recovery after that.

Fifty-five years ago, the headline in the paper about my cardiac arrest would have been "Speaker Collapses and Dies." Instead, the headline was "Doctor Credits South

Bend Firefighter with Saving His Life" (*South Bend Tribune*, November 5, 2010).

Resuscitation for a cardiac arrest is fraught with the high probability of failure. In my situation, all the right people were there who knew what to do and responded quickly and appropriately. Response time is critical. Minutes and seconds count. With each minute of delay before starting resuscitation, the chance of survival decreases by 15 percent. Even under optimal conditions many people do not survive. Overall the survival rate *for people whose out-of-hospital cardiac arrest was witnessed* is 14 percent or about one in seven. However, only one half of those that survive—one in fourteen—regain their pre-arrest neurological status.

> *It may be an advantage to know*
> *you are facing your terminal illness.*

How one dies may be beyond the individual's control. Death may come within a few minutes of a catastrophic event, or it might occur after many months or years of cancer or other lingering or recurring illness. There are dozens of diseases that remain incurable, such as Alzheimer's, ALS (Lou Gehrig's disease), melanoma, or emphysema (COPD). People who have an incurable illness face the reality that their disease will likely be terminal.

Since we can't get out of this life alive anyhow, it may be an advantage to know you are facing your terminal illness; it provides time and space to prepare for a good death which reflects the values and theology that have guided your life.

A CONVERSATION WITH FATHER KILIAN ON DYING

In the fall of 2011, I spent four months working on this manuscript as a resident scholar at the Collegeville Institute, an ecumenical program of St. Benedict's Monastery in

Collegeville, Minnesota. Among the numerous helpful and inspiring contacts was Father Kilian, a ninety-year-old monk whose office was a few steps down the hall from mine. Over the weeks, we had many delightful conversations ranging from our childhood origins to our destination after death.

Kilian: I grew up in a large Catholic family. Life was hard, especially for my mother because my father traveled and was gone most of the time. The church was the center of our life. As a teenager, I was responsible to light the fire early on Sunday mornings to warm the church in time for services. I decided I wanted to be a monk early in life and was eventually accepted by the Benedictines.

Glen: I grew up in a large Mennonite family during the Great Depression. Life was hard, especially for my mother with nine children in thirteen years. We were poor but we didn't know it because all our neighbors were in a similar situation. Our Mennonite church community was the center of our social and religious life. By age thirteen, I knew I wanted to be a medical doctor but had no idea how to get the money for the required education.

Kilian, we are ninety and seventy-nine years old. Chances are, the next big transition for both of us is dying. I want to talk more about that.

Kilian: In our community of monks, it's an advantage to have monks dying in our midst. If nothing else, it tells us, "Look Buster, it's going to end." Dying is viewed as part of living.

Glen: When I grew up, dying was a hush-hush subject, spoken of only in whispers when the children weren't around. I unexpectedly and suddenly needed to face the end of my life at the time of my first heart attack in Calcutta. That first night in the hospital, I realized that I could die and was entirely at peace with that possibility.

Kilian: At my dying time, I visualize what is customary: the abbot will post a note suggesting that monks come and give their blessing. Then the abbot will come in and anoint me with monks present in my room and others lining the hallway outside my door. If the abbot came into my room and said, "Kilian you are about to go to God. You can go with great confidence for you don't go empty handed: you go with your national and international ecumenical dialogue and your books on theology and poetry." If the abbot says that to me, he will send me into unmitigated despair.

I know that my good works are pleasing to God. The apostle Paul says in Romans that God "'will repay each person according to what they have done.' To those who by persistence in doing good seek glory, honor and immortality, he will give eternal life."[1] We believe that good works are rewarded—repaid. But I know that all my works are flawed with pride and ambition and that is not where I place my hope. I want the abbot to hold up the crucifix before me and say, "Place all your hope in the death and resurrection of Jesus Christ." Then I can die with great confidence and peace.

Glen: I haven't really thought about what I present to God. What I do know is that I have tried to follow the teachings and the way of Jesus. For me, spirituality means to be "imitators of God" like it says in Ephesians[2]—to try to take on the attributes of God. This has immense implications on how I relate to others who are also created in the image of God. If I am serious about being an imitator of God, it will fully guide all my actions.

I have confidence that at the time of my death, God will lovingly receive me into the Divine Presence. On two

1. Romans 2:6-7.
2. Ephesians 5:1.

occasions, with close friends near death, I prayed just that at their bedsides, expressing my confidence that a loving and forgiving God would receive them. I believe the same for me when my time comes.

In my community it is not uncommon to be anointed. My father, when he knew death was near, was anointed to "clear the way to the other side." From that experience and others, I see anointing as a time when family and friends gather to witness to God's grace and forgiveness, and to affirm the life of the dying person.

Kilian: It is important to grapple with death. There's a lot of consolation and strength with the awareness that we step from death into life. A monk's life is a life of prayer. Saturday mornings are a special time of reflection for me. During that time I seek God using the monastic tools available to me. I gather up my life and offer it to God. I tell God that I want him to have everything in my life. I sought God, but in fact I did not give him everything.

When I think of meeting God, my template is the prodigal son who is walking home in disgrace. As he is walking, he is practicing the speech he will give to his father. While he is still a long way off, his father sees him and comes running out of the house, laughing and crying. The son starts his speech and the father hushes him and will not let him finish. The father accepts him back with great joy. It's not presumptuous to feel confident in that acceptance. In just this way, God will accept us.

Confession is an enormous gift, especially when one is facing death. Sacramental grace is powerful. In a confession, I approach God with my messes, like a child making mud pies for their grandpa, decorating them with stones and baking them in the sun. As I offer my messes to God, I am not going to brag, for it is indeed messy, but it's *my* mess and I offer it to him.

Glen: In my discussions with clergy of differing religious traditions, they all talked about the importance of confession at the end of life to receive forgiveness and release. I like the mental picture of approaching God with my messes. I also have confidence that God will accept me with my failings.

Have you given thought about how much care you want to get when you are dying?

Kilian: I haven't given that much thought. My community of monks makes that decision for me. I would say this: don't waste money on me. I don't want surgery for cancer. An ideal approach for me would be to make me comfortable and let me go.

Glen: My primary community is my family. We have talked in some detail about how much care I want to receive. I made it clear that I want my life extended only if I have the prospect of a decent quality of living. If I can't relate in meaningful ways to those around me, I don't want life-support measures to extend my life. I also don't want to create hardships, financial or otherwise, for my family in my time of dying.

Kilian: I have had a good life. I really love my life and I love my work. It is very satisfying, *very satisfying.* I came from a large family with seven boys and one girl. My sister said, "Kilian, of all of us, you made the most of your life." I don't believe that for a minute; they raised families. Life as a monk is a piece of cake compared to that. There have been marvelous opportunities for me to pray with my conferees and alone, to be educated, and to participate in international dialogues between the Vatican and worldwide churches. I am deeply grateful to God for calling me to the monastic life. It is an eternal gift.

Glen: I also look back on my life with satisfaction and gratefulness. I feel I have been able to contribute toward a better life for those around me, those close in like my family, the patients that I cared for, and those far from home like the poor people from Haiti to Calcutta to Phnom Penh. In retrospect, it seems a remarkable journey for a farm boy who grew up during the Depression with limited prospects.

Kilian, our lives have more similarities than I imagined. We both grew up in large families where faith and the religious community were central. We both took seriously the need to contribute to those around us. Despite our differing circumstances and the traditional gulf between Catholics and Mennonites, we share so much in our outlook and understanding of what is to come in the next life.

Kilian: I have never had a conversation like this before.

Glen: Neither have I.

MEDICAL INTERVENTIONS

Many people do not have the luxury of a leisurely and reflective conversation about dying. When sudden catastrophic illness strikes, there is no time to think and prepare for the inevitable decisions that are required in the course of end-of-life medical care.

In the following story, Ezra suffered a severe heart attack followed by a seemingly endless parade of life-support measures. As you read this story, I hope you can sense the frustration and tension that persisted for Ezra's family over the period of months before he died.

Ezra's life had followed a trajectory of marriage, education, and business management, more education, eventually attaining a PhD, and landing in the place of his first love—teaching university students. At age sixty-two, he anticipated continuing teaching until retirement.

On a fall morning as he bicycled to work, he suddenly passed out and was found by other bikers lying at the edge of the trail. The EMTs were called and subsequent tests showed that he had a massive heart attack. He was taken for emergency coronary bypass surgery, but the damage to his heart was so severe that he required a heart pump assist to maintain his blood pressure and circulation. Ezra had two more surgeries in the next week due to bleeding. Because of these continued complications, he was transferred to a larger hospital three hours away from his home.

"I didn't want to feel we had pulled the plug."

He continued on a breathing machine (ventilator) and was maintained in a medically induced coma. After seven weeks, doctors removed the heart pump and ventilator. He was able to only speak in a whisper because of damage to his larynx from the breathing tube. He had no short-term memory, continually asking the same questions about where he was and what had happened. A brain scan showed no evidence of a stroke. His kidneys failed and he was started on dialysis three times a week. He eventually began eating and was started on physical therapy. In the three months after his heart attack, he never regained his short-term memory.

After three months in the larger hospital, Ezra was transferred to the hospital in their hometown. Eventually, he was placed in hospice care and died from fluid buildup in his lungs from his failing heart. Ezra's wife, Sue, wondered if she was "pulling the plug."

During this entire time, Sue stayed three hours away from home near the hospital and separated from her friends at church. Their children were with her much of the time, but she sorely missed the close contact with her church community.

Two years later, as Sue reviewed what happened, she recalled the many decisions that needed to be made. She felt these decisions were made without discussion of the hoped-for outcomes. One of the many decisions was when Ezra developed kidney failure and the doctors recommended dialysis. Due to his failing heart, there was real question about the advisability of proceeding with dialysis. Her daughter told Sue, "We can't just let him die."

Ezra and Sue had completed advance directives with specific limitations but had not discussed them with their three children.

In recounting this story, Sue said repeatedly, "I needed my church family to help me make decisions." She felt alone with the tremendous weight of these decisions. She said, "I was made to feel by the doctors that if we didn't go ahead at each step, that I would be taking Ezra's life. I didn't want to feel we had pulled the plug. I was never given the option to *not* do something."

Life support measures used for Ezra included

- emergency medical technicians (EMTs),

- a heart defibrillator,

- an endotracheal tube,

- bypass surgery,

- cardiopulmonary bypass (heart-lung machine),

- a ventricular assist device (heart pump),

- a ventilator,

- a medically-induced coma,

- kidney dialysis, and

- a hospice program.

Ezra's story illustrates the extent to which medical decisions affected the course of the remainder of his life. A cascade of events like this can take on a life of its own. Ezra's wife and family felt there was no time or space given to consider the larger issues; rather, the course of events moved inexorably onward, always in the hope that the next intervention would turn the corner and restore Ezra to a full life.

In contrast to fifty years ago, most people today don't "just up and die"—we manage their deaths. Along the way in the process of dying, Ezra's family made multiple decisions, each with a struggle to understand the implications and advisability.

In hindsight, it would have been appropriate to ask questions: What would Ezra want? How do Ezra's advance directives apply here? What if we *don't* do the next thing advised? What are the chances of a full neurologic recovery including short-term memory? When dialysis is being considered, what is the prospect for a decent quality of life?

WHO IS IN CHARGE HERE?

The following story of Henry, an elderly man, as told by his son, illustrates how Henry's medical care moved relentlessly forward, ignoring the wishes of the dying patient and his quality of life.

A week after we celebrated Dad's ninety-seventh birthday, he tripped and fell, fracturing five vertebrae in his neck. He was taken from the local hospital to a more distant medical center. Ten days later he was released to a rehabilitation center near his home, to continue recuperation.

For the next nine weeks Dad was shuttled between the rehab center and back to the local hospital with additional complications. As time went by, the hospital stays became longer and the time in the rehab center shorter.

Dad's condition was complicated by congestive heart failure of several years' duration. Twice he developed severe infections but managed to pull through. As he went from one crisis to another, specialists were called, including an orthopedist, an internist, a cardiologist, and a nephrologist. Each specialist addressed their particular organ system, ordering more tests, medicines, and treatment procedures. Repeatedly, we observed that the doctors were not talking with each other.

Dad became increasingly frustrated by all the medical procedures. Dad and Mom had living wills and had assigned durable power of attorney to their son who lived nearby. As a family, we made certain that the lead physician was informed of Dad's clear instruction to take "no heroic measures" on his behalf.

Dad was lucid throughout. He kept saying, "I'm ready to die. I don't want to be subjected to these costly and onerous medical procedures when the prospect of regaining any quality of life is minimal. Please let me go."

Finally, two and a half months after the injury, the lead doctor told Dad and the family that his congestive heart condition had progressed to the point where nothing further could be done for him. The tests and procedures ended only when the doctors decided they could end.

My sister and her husband drove from Seattle, arriving at nine o'clock that evening. The family gathered around Dad. He recited one of his favorite Psalms: "Bless the Lord, O my soul . . ."[3] and lifted his hands in final benediction on those present. He died peacefully several hours later.

---

3. Psalm 103 (KJV).

There are specific times during the course of an illness or injury when patients and their families make critical decisions that set the course of medical treatment. In the preceding story, Henry was pleading for no more tests and asking that the treatments be curtailed. Following are a number of decision points:

1. "He tripped and fell, fracturing five vertebrae in his neck." *The decision to call the EMT squad was clearly indicated because Henry was in severe pain and unable to move. In other situations, with a little thought, the patient and family will realize that their situation does not require emergency treatment. It is important to understand that calling the EMTs is implied consent to medical treatment.*

2. "He was taken from the local hospital to a more distant medical center." *Henry was moved to a more distant hospital to provide more specialized care. This move made it impossible for his primary physician to remain involved in his care and likely resulted in less control over medical decisions. The fact that Henry and his family agreed to make the move was implied consent for a higher level of specialized care and technology.*

3. "Specialists were called . . . [who] addressed their particular organ system . . . we observed that the doctors were not talking with each other." *The role of a specialist is to look at the patient through the lens of his/her specialty. The family noted that the heart doctor, the lung doctor, the kidney doctor, and the bone doctor were not talking to each other. At this point, the primary doctor who knows the patient's wishes is frequently no longer involved in providing care.*

4. "Dad and Mom had living wills and had assigned durable power of attorney to their son who lived nearby." *Henry and his wife had properly prepared advance directives and appointed a PAHCD (power of attorney for healthcare*

decisions). All too often at the time of an emergency, the advance directives and previous discussions regarding any limitations of care are forgotten or ignored.

5. "Dad became increasingly frustrated by all the medical procedures. . . . He kept saying, 'I'm ready to die.' . . . nothing further could be done for him." *Despite the best efforts of the cardiologist, internist, orthopedist, and nephrologist to squeeze better function out of their organ of interest, they now had nothing more to offer. Up to this point, no one, not any of the doctors or the PAHCD, had stepped forward with any discussion of limits to his care.*

> *The family is left to wonder if they had done right by their father.*

6. "The tests and procedures ended only when the doctors decided they could end." *The family was left to wonder if they had done right by their father.*

A GOOD DEATH

I heard more end-of-life stories—both good and bad—from friends and family members about how a parent had died. One of the good stories I personally observed was that of my oldest sister, Lois, which stands in contrast to the two stories above.

At seventy-four years of age, Lois looked with satisfaction on her family of six daughters and one son, all now serving their communities in social service, teaching, or healthcare. Times were not always easy. At age fifty-two, out of financial necessity, she completed her training as a practical nurse in order to contribute to the family income. For more than twenty years, she worked in the newborn nursery of the local hospital. She retired from nursing and looked forward to spending more time with her family scattered over six states.

After retirement, Lois, always alert and engaged, began to have times when she was confused. At a church meal, she couldn't remember how to use a knife and fork. Her doctor treated her symptoms without a specific diagnosis. Later, she was unable to talk when she awakened in the morning. Her family took her to an emergency room where a CT of her brain revealed a tumor. Lois's daughter Renee remembers the compassion of the doctor who broke the news that she had a brain tumor. He told her that he too had a progressive disease and understood the shock of this news. He told Lois, "We are on the same path but you will get there before I do."

The same day they took her to a larger hospital where a biopsy was scheduled. On the way to that hospital, Lois repeatedly said she wasn't ready to die: that she had accomplished so little in her lifetime and needed more time. When they arrived at the hospital, Lois was being wheeled down the hall when a young nurse stopped her and knelt down beside her with tears streaming. She told Lois how much she had meant to her as a young single mother. It had been Lois who encouraged her to get nurse's training.

The biopsy confirmed a highly malignant brain tumor. When told about the diagnosis, Lois said one word: "Bummer." Later she said she was afraid to leave the family. She had always been the organizer and she kept her well-meaning and hard-working husband organized.

From that time onward, Lois prepared to die. The family explored possible treatment but they were warned that any surgical treatment would leave her unresponsive and unable to talk. Doctors at a university cancer clinic held out no hope for cure. Doctors entered her into an experimental program of radiation and chemotherapy. In a few weeks, it was clear that the treatment wasn't working and was only making her sicker. Lois and her family decided to leave the hospital and spend her remaining days at home.

In the next weeks Lois remained fully aware and responsive. During this time the entire family gathered and made a video recording of Lois recalling times when the children were small and happy family memories. In the middle of the video, filmed outside their home, a deer walked past within view of the camera as if to herald life and vitality.

The family has no regrets.

The time came when someone needed to be with Lois constantly, and the family set up a schedule so that two people were with her at all times. When she had repeated seizures, a daughter slept on each side of her to prevent her from falling out of bed. Hospice nurses visited regularly.

During the last weeks of her life, Lois described vivid dreams, including one restless night when she dreamed she was helping her mother prepare a banquet table in heaven. On another occasion, she was looking intently at the ceiling of the room, and when asked what she saw, she said she was looking at the face of Jesus.

In her last two weeks of life, Lois was unresponsive. The family took turns reading and singing to her. When the church choir came to the bedside to sing familiar songs, all were amazed when they realized that Lois was singing along, harmonizing in her usual alto role. She died at night, surrounded by her children singing "Jesus Loves Me."

The family has no regrets about the last weeks of their mother's life. I observed the family as they cared for Lois over several months until she died. It was a good death. Several things stood out:

- *Get a proper diagnosis if at all possible.* When Lois's symptoms appeared, the family took the necessary steps to get a proper diagnosis, including a biopsy. Being certain of the diagnosis diminished the possibility of doubts and second-guessing. Frustrations can run high when there is no diagnosis to explain the symptoms. It is often a relief to have a specific diagnosis even if the prognosis is poor.

- *Explore treatment options.* The children in this family talked to their doctors and explored the Internet for options for treatment.

- *Maintain a realistic attitude toward interventions.* When it became clear that the only possible treatment was ineffective, their attention turned toward providing the best possible experience for Lois and for the family. They avoided treatment that had little chance of being effective "just to do *something.*"

- *Plan for the time remaining.* After a brief hospitalization, the family took Lois home and made plans with the help of hospice to care for her there. They concentrated on making the best use of the time that Lois had remaining.

- *Organize the caregiving.* Lois was blessed with an attentive and loving husband and seven children. All of her six daughters, son, and daughter-in-law shared responsibility in caring for Lois. With the help of hospice, they were able to keep her at home, fulfilling her wish that she would die there.

- *Create good memories.* They intentionally spent time designed to create memories for the grandchildren. While Lois was yet able, they videotaped her reminiscences that spanned the lifetime of her family for a permanent record.

- *Walking this journey together was a bonding time for family members.* As I observed the family going through the process of caring for Lois, I saw their affection and trust of one another that led to easy and open communication. After Lois died, they truly celebrated her life, unencumbered with residual misunderstandings or feelings of remorse. In their family gatherings, the memories of their mother's last days are easily recalled and discussed.

I now know my "terminal illness."

How and when I die may be beyond my control. However, it is likely that I now know my "terminal illness." After my cardiac arrest, I noticed that when I try to walk as fast as before, I become short of breath, with weakness in my legs and a tendency for my legs to swell—all symptoms of a failing heart. And indeed, my cardiologist made it official with the diagnosis of congestive heart failure (CHF). So with a heart weakened by two heart attacks, dependent on a pacemaker, the diagnosis of CHF, and after two cardiac arrests, I can no longer ignore the fact that my life will be shortened. Knowing that, I have become serious about making the plans that will ease the tension—for myself and my family—of making the necessary healthcare decisions as my end approaches.

QUESTIONS AND SUGGESTIONS FOR DISCUSSION:

1. What is a sudden death?

2. Why does the author state that "it may be an advantage to know you are facing your terminal illness"?

3. What were the critical medical care decisions made in the care of Henry?

4. Review and discuss the issues that made the family wonder if "they had done right by their father."

5. Identify the medical care decisions made for Lois's care.

6. Review and discuss the seven things that contributed to Lois's "good" death.

Three

The Way We Die Has Changed

The way people die remains in the memory of those who live on. —Dame Cecily Saunders, founder of the modern hospice movement

DYING HAS CHANGED

As a boy growing up in Ohio, I recall that when a neighbor died my mother asked why and no one really knew. He "just up and died." There was so much that was mysterious and unknowable. People just did that sometimes. These days, dying is not so simple. Dying has become a *process* with multiple options to consider in the diagnosis and treatment. Several generations ago, life support machines were not available. Typically, an aging person gradually became frailer and eventually took to their bed and died. The moment of death was clear—the heartbeat and breathing stopped.

> *Dying has become a process with multiple options to consider.*

Sixteen percent of us die suddenly within minutes of the onset of a catastrophic event like a heart attack, stroke, or accident.[1] The other 84 percent die in stages due to aging or chronic disease such as diabetes, heart disease, lung disease, or cancer. We begin dying when organ systems no longer do what they are intended to do—the heart pumps less blood, the lungs are less efficient in exchanging life-giving oxygen for carbon dioxide, toxins accumulate in the blood because the kidneys no longer effectively filter the blood, or our brain doesn't work and we've lost the ability to think and remember.

> *It's amazing to recall what we didn't have seventy-five years ago.*

Today, we have life support machines that can pace the heart, breathe for the patient, and cleanse the blood of toxins. As a consequence, the time it takes to die is prolonged, and often death happens only when the family and medical care-takers decide it should. The dying process requires decisions on the part of the patient and family that will determine the quality of dying. The thesis of this book is that *everyone deserves a good death and a good death requires planning.*

MIRACLE DRUGS AND MEDICAL SCANS

Looking back to my childhood, the changes in healthcare are breathtaking. Dying at that time was unencumbered by beeping monitors, feeding tubes, or the rhythm of a breathing machine. More common was the Norman Rockwell–like picture of the dying person in his own bed, at home, surrounded by his family, a doctor standing by who has done what he can to comfort the patient. The dying parent turns to his family with a final goodbye and blessing. This scene becomes sacred as final words are remembered and passed on to friends and relatives.

---

1. Myron L. Weisfeldt and Susan J. Zieman, "Advances in the Prevention and Treatment of Cardiovascular Disease," Health Affairs 26, no. 1 (January 2007), http://content.healthaffairs.org/content/26/1/25.full?sid= 65062a95-5181-4bfd-a573-bba8fcb0d92a.

It is amazing to recall what we *didn't have* seventy-five years ago. When my mother gave birth to my youngest brother, she developed the dreaded puerperal fever that killed young mothers for centuries. Before the invention of the microscope and the identification of microorganisms, 20 to 25 percent of mothers died from the postpartum fever. Without knowledge of antisepsis, doctors and midwives spread the disease from one mother to another. In 1843, Oliver Wendell Holmes, suspecting the cause of the disease, wrote that he would prefer that his family be delivered unattended in a manger to avoid being exposed to "the vapors of this pitiless disease."

Even after the knowledge of sterile techniques had advanced, once the infection took hold, little could be done to avoid a tragic end with the death of a woman in her prime leaving another newborn motherless.

My mother's situation was desperate, and nine small children, including my newborn brother, faced growing up without a mother. On a Sunday morning, as she went to surgery, the congregation of West Clinton Church prayed that her life would be spared. Whether due to the prayers of the faithful or the recently developed sulfa medicine that the doctor managed to secure, my mother pulled through. The sulfa medicine was thought to be a miracle drug. We began to hear a new word—*antibiotic*.

Sulfa and penicillin were the harbingers of thousands of various medicines with an effectiveness that we take for granted. We now have medicines to treat conditions as familiar as high blood pressure, as fearful as cancer, as mundane as male-pattern hair loss, as common as diabetes, as prevalent as depression, and if one judges by the number of advertisements, the most dreaded erectile dysfunction.

It's amazing to consider all the advances in diagnosis and treatment in my lifetime. I first heard about cardiopulmonary resuscitation (CPR) in 1958 in my second year of medical school. Doctors discovered that in the event of a heart attack, the injured heart was prone to lapse into a fatal rhythm. In some cases, heart function could be restored if the erratic rhythm—ventricular fibrillation—was treated with an electric shock. A number of patients lived for years after the cardiac arrest that formerly would have been fatal.

The need for intensive treatment and observation after a heart attack led to establishing special units, commonly called intensive care or cardiac care units. The advances in technology such as ventilators to assist breathing required more specially trained nurses and technicians.

In the 1970s, the ability to diagnose problems took a leap forward with the invention of the ultrasound machine. In the next several decades, researchers invented CT scans (computerized tomography) and MRI (magnetic resonance imaging). Now we are able to obtain images from body cavities where before doctors made educated guesses of the likely diagnosis. Because of the improved ability to diagnose, exploratory surgery has become much less common.

To a person living fifty years ago, the advances in medicine of today would be truly awe-inspiring. Today, a mother no longer dreads the onslaught of measles, whooping cough, scarlet fever, or pneumonia in her children. Even with wild stretches of imagination, fifty years ago, a mother would be unable to imagine joint replacement, organ transplants, endoscopic surgery, gene manipulation, or a thousand other tests and treatments. These developments along with improved nutrition and sanitation have provided a longer and more comfortable life. In the last thirty years, average life span increased 5.0 years (from 73.7 to 78.7) in the United States[2] and 6.2 years (from 74.9 to 81.1) in Canada.[3]

2. "Life Expectancy at Birth by Race and Sex, 1930–2010," *Information Please Database* (Source: National Center for Health Statistics, www.cdc.gov/nchs), http://www.infoplease.com/ipa/A0005148.html.

3. Human Resources and Skills Development Canada, http://www4.hrsdc.gc.ca/.3ndic.1t.4r@-eng.jsp?iid=3.

THE LACK OF HEALTHCARE

Millions of North Americans and billions around the world suffer from the lack of even the most rudimentary medical care. Many of them die a painful death—*not* a good death.

In 1979 to 1981, I spent a total of six months in Egypt teaching medical students and hospital staff internal medicine. My arrival had been advertised in *Al-Ahram,* the major Cairo newspaper, and my days were filled with teaching rounds and patient consultations.

One afternoon, a man arrived with his fifteen-year-old son. They had traveled a long distance by oxcart and bus from his remote village to the south. His son had been ill for a number of months and had already seen doctors in other clinics. In a last-ditch effort to help his son, the father brought him to the "American" doctor.

As was common among village families, this son, alone among his siblings, was sent to school to get an education in the hope that he would find good employment and lift the family out of poverty. The boy's jaundiced skin and protruding abdomen told me he had been sick a long time. The youth had advanced liver cirrhosis and failure caused by schistosomiasis due to a parasite that enters the bodies of people who swim in the canals. Thirty years ago there was no treatment.

While I was examining the boy, I became keenly aware of the father standing nearby, expectantly and eagerly awaiting the words that would assure him of his son's recovery. I struggled to find the words I knew I needed to say. As gently as I could through a translator, I gave the man the bad news. The look of hope on the father's face dissolved into paroxysms of grief. For years thereafter, I wept with each retelling of that story.

Most of us in North America have access to medical care and the advantages of decent sanitation and do not suffer from the lack of healthcare. On the contrary, in our time of dying we may suffer from *too much medical care*.

TOO MUCH MEDICAL CARE

In the last few years, when I presented my views on healthcare, I have been saying that *more* healthcare is not necessarily *better* healthcare. The authors of an article in a recent issue of a major medical journal state that "There is widespread agreement that more is not always better in health care. Doing more can harm patients, generate excess costs, and defy patient preferences."[4]

More healthcare can harm patients, generate excess costs, and defy patient preferences.

The *Archives of Internal Medicine* now has a regular feature article that cites the evidence where the risk of a treatment or diagnostic procedure outweighs the benefit. In 2012, a multi-specialty team of medical experts identified thirty-seven tests or treatments that are harmful or have no proven value.[5] Doctors representing all major specialties continue to add to the list of tests now in common use that are useless.

The *Archives* reported on a survey of 627 doctors who reported that in their own practices, 42 percent of their patients received too much care.[6] This over-testing and over-treatment does nothing to improve the quality of care.

---

4. Allison Lipitz-Snyderman, PhD, and Peter B. Bach, MD, MAPP, "Overuse of Health Care Services When Less is More . . . More or Less," *JAMA Intern Med.* 173, no. 14 (2013):1277–78, http://archinte.jamanetwork.com/article.aspx?articleID=1691771.

5. Amir Qaseem, MD, PhD et al., "Thirty-Seven Clinical Situations in Which a Test Does Not Reflect High-Value Care," *Annals of Internal Medicine,* 156, no. 2 (January 2012), http://annals.org/article.aspx?articleid=1033300.

6. Brenda E. Sirovich, MD et al., "Too Little? Too Much? Primary Care Physicians' Views on US Health Care," *Archives of Internal Medicine* 171, no. 17 (2011):1582–85.

It is proper to question the need for diagnostic tests, including scans. Medical scanning is the fastest growing segment of medical care. A *New York Times* editorial states that scans, including CT, MRI, and PET (positron emission tomography) scans, are done ninety-five million times each year to the cost of one hundred billion dollars.[7] Increasingly, doctors own their own scan machines and self-refer, thereby increasing their income. Fully qualified radiologists estimate that 20 to 50 percent of the scans done today are of inferior quality and "useless."

Further, tests may be done because it is easier—for the doctor—to repeat a test than find the result of the last one. There are a number of questions physicians need to ask themselves before ordering a test:[8]

1. If the test was done previously, what is the indication for repeating it now?

2. Was the test done elsewhere, and if so, can I get the result from that source?

3. How accurate is the proposed test?

4. What are the consequences of a false positive test?

5. Will the test result change how I care for this patient?

6. Am I ordering this test out of fear of a lawsuit?

7. Am I ordering this test primarily to reassure the patient? Can the patient be reassured by further explanation?

Public information on medicines and procedures gives the impression that there is no end to the conditions that medicine

---

7. Gina Kolata, "Good or Useless, Medical Scans Cost the Same," *New York Times*, March 1, 2009, http://www.nytimes.com/2009/03/02/health/02scans.html.

8. Adapted from the editorial "High Value Testing Begins with a Few Simple Questions," *Annals of Internal Medicine* 156, no. 2 (January 17, 2012):162.

and technology can cure. So, as consumers of healthcare we are convinced that many of the solutions to our life problems can be found in pills or treatments. H. Gilbert Welch et al., in their article "What's Making Us Sick Is an Epidemic of Diagnoses" (*New York Times*, January 2, 2007), said in part:

> This epidemic [of diagnoses] is a threat to your health. It has two distinct sources. One is the "medicalization" of everyday life. Most of us experience physical or emotional sensations we don't like, and in the past, this was considered a part of life. Increasingly, however, such sensations are considered symptoms of disease. Everyday experiences like insomnia, sadness, twitchy legs and impaired sex drive now become diagnoses: sleep disorder, depression, restless leg syndrome and sexual dysfunction.

Further, we believe that more care is always better—if one test is good, two are better. Coupled with this mindset is a healthcare system that is only too willing to respond with more tests, more treatments, and the newest and most expensive medicine, for in doing so it enhances their bottom line. With this set of conditions, the healthcare system becomes a veritable machine, a machine that has no effective braking system to slow its runaway prices. In Canada the pressure to over treat is lessened, due in part to lower threats of lawsuits and tighter government regulation within the National Health Service.

> Lawrence took his wife, Marg, to the ER after a fall in her home. She was not unconscious but had a laceration above the eye that needed sutures. After the ER doctor completed the suturing, he prepared to send Marg for a CT scan. Lawrence, surprised by the plan for the CT, told the doctor they would watch Marg through the night and bring her back for the scan if there was any question about her condition. The doctor insisted and the scan showed no abnormalities.

Knowing who reaps financial rewards from this simple transaction is helpful in understanding how the healthcare system works. The hospital benefits since CT scans, MRIs, and X-rays are a profit center for hospitals. These tests provide income to the technician who does the testing, the radiologist who interprets the test, and indirectly to the medical supplier who manufactures the diagnostic machines and provides the operating supplies. The contract for ER doctors in some hospitals provides for a base pay with added income based on the number of tests she or he orders. Furthermore, people who "paid good money" for health insurance see no reason for restraint in its use.

The healthcare system becomes a veritable machine without a braking system to slow runaway prices.

The total cost of Medicare in the United States is about one trillion dollars per year. Are these dollars well spent? Consider the following: (1) Twenty-five percent of all Medicare dollars are spent in the last year of life with 40 percent of *that* amount spent in the last thirty days. (2) Twenty-five percent of diagnostic tests and treatment for Medicare patients are considered useless and a disservice to the patient.[9] (3) Seventy percent of patients say they want to die at home, yet only 40 percent do so.[10] (4) The cost of healthcare is 35 percent less when the doctors are salaried rather than working on a production basis.[11] (5) The World Health Organization rates the United States thirty-eighth in the world in the quality of healthcare.[12]

---

9. Ashish K Jha et al., "Improving Safety and Eliminating Redundant Tests: Cutting Costs in U.S. Hospitals," *Health Affairs* 28, no. 5 (2009), http://content.healthaffairs.org/content/28/5/1475.full.pdf+html.

10. Dying Matters Coalition: Frequently Asked Questions, http://dyingmatters.org/page/frequently-asked-questions.

11. Gardiner Harris, "Hospital Savings: Salaries for Doctors, Not Fees," *New York Times*, July 24, 2009, http://www.nytimes.com/2009/07/25/health/policy/25doctors.html?_r=0.

12. Wikipedia, "World Health Organization ranking of health systems," http://en.wikipedia.org/wiki/World_Health_Organization_ranking_of_health_systems.

THE WAY THE DOCTOR SEES IT

Regardless of the age of the patient, the doctor's first instinct, reinforced by years of training, is to keep the patient alive. In achieving this goal, the doctor has available a vast array of technology and a virtual army of technicians prepared to apply their training and tools. The doctor, as the commander of this platoon, writes the initial orders that get things moving and follows through with the necessary measures to return the patient back to health. Traditionally, the expectation of patients and their families is that the healthcare system will carry on the fight until all scientific options are exhausted. When, despite all efforts, the patient dies, it is often seen as failure.

As the doctor cares for the patient, she or he must carefully document the rationale for the care based on scientific principles and the current standard of care. In the medical climate of today, as she orders diagnostic tests, procedures, and treatment, somewhere in her subliminal mind she will be aware of the need to protect herself in case of a lawsuit. To achieve this, she needs to anticipate what she may be asked on the witness stand in a malpractice suit. Did she order the proper tests? Was the treatment appropriate? If the treatment was not effective, why not?

A doctor dreads the prospect of being dragged into court with public allegations that he or she mistreated a patient. Understandably, doctors try to protect themselves against that possibility. Seventy-two orthopedic surgeons graded themselves on the medical scans they ordered for 2,068 patients. Their conclusion: *Twenty percent of the tests were not necessary* to make a diagnosis but were ordered to cover themselves in case of a lawsuit.[13]

---

13. "Report: 20% of Orthopedic Surgeons' Imaging Orders Are Defensive," February 28, 2011, http://www.physiciansweekly.com/blog/2011/02/28/report-orthopedic-surgeons-motivated-by-defensive-medicine-in-20-of-imaging-orders/.

A recent study[14] of over forty thousand physicians in all specialties showed that the risk of a lawsuit before the age of sixty-five for physicians in a high-risk category (neurosurgery, orthopedics, and obstetrics) is 99 percent. The comparable risk for low-risk physicians (family practice, pediatrics, and psychiatry) is 75 percent. A malpractice suit places significant emotional stress on the doctor in addition to potential loss of income and reputation.

Twenty percent of the tests were not necessary to make a diagnosis

The cost of settling malpractice lawsuits in the United States is 1.7 percent of the total healthcare cost and about sixteen dollars per person per year. The cost of defensive medicine (tests and treatments ordered by the doctor because of the fear of a lawsuit) is estimated to increase the cost to 9 percent of the total. In Canada, malpractice lawsuits account for 0.27 percent of the total cost and four dollars per person per year. Overall, there is about 3.5 times the number of lawsuits in the United States compared to Canada.[15]

Open conversation that builds trust between doctor and patient will reduce the need to practice defensive medicine, as illustrated in my friend Paul's story:

> Last week, I went to the doctor for my annual physical exam. Everything checked out well except he told me there were red blood cells in my urine. I am on Coumadin because of a previous problem with venous thrombosis and blood clots to my lungs. I assumed the red blood cells could be related to the Coumadin.

14. Anupam B. Jena, MD, PhD et al., "Malpractice Risk According to Physician Specialty," *New England Journal of Medicine* (August 18, 2011), 365:629–36.

15. See appendix 2 for a more detailed comparison of the U.S. and Canadian healthcare systems.

The doctor explained that it may be a serious problem or nothing bad. It was clear to me that the wheels were turning in the doctor's head, trying to decide what to do next. Finally, I said to him, "Look, I won't sue you. Can't we just recheck the urine in a week?" The doctor immediately decided against getting further tests including X-rays. One week later there was no evidence of blood in the urine and no further tests were necessary.

Paul recognized the "elephant in the room"—the need to cover all the bases because of the fear of a lawsuit—that allowed a frank conversation and a less invasive way of dealing with the problem. Importantly, Paul's healthcare actually improved because X-rays were *not done*, eliminating unnecessary radiation and the possibility of a reaction to the dye.

Under the U.S. healthcare system, the private practice doctor also becomes an entrepreneur. The expenses of a medical office must be met, office building mortgage and employees paid, expensive equipment purchased and maintained, utility bills and malpractice insurance premiums paid. If the doctor is under thirty-five, he is likely paying off the cost of medical school education—the median education debt for the 86 percent of medical school graduates who are indebted was $170,000 in 2012.[16] A 2012 survey of Canadian medical students found that 82 percent expected to have debt after their training is complete. Of these students, one-third expects a debt in excess of $100,000 and 19 percent over $160,000.[17] All

---

16. Association of American Medical Colleges, *Physician Education Debt and the Cost to Attend Medical School: 2012 Update* (February 2013), https://www.aamc.org/download/328322/data/statedebtreport.pdf.

17. Canadian Collaborative Centre for Physician Resources, "Off to Work I Owe! Results of the 2012 National Physician Survey of Medical Students and Residents," accessed August 22, 2013, http://nationalphysiciansurvey.ca/wp-content/uploads/2013/03/C3PR-Bulletin-StudentResidentDebt-201303-EN.pdf.

of these expenses can be met only as she works and generates charges. If she goes on holiday, the bills still come in.

In an extended illness, multiple specialists will be called with each focusing on their area of expertise. These specialists may not talk to each other, leaving no one to look to the holistic needs of the patient. After my cardiac arrest, two cardiologists addressed the needs of my ailing heart. They reported their plans for diagnostic testing and findings to me. I appreciated their expertise and thoroughness. At the same time, I found myself wanting a doctor to look me in the eyes and ask, "And how are *you* doing?" I am more than the circulation of the blood through coronary arteries and more than the way my heart was being paced. The essence of me is still there with emotional, social, and spiritual needs.

THE WAY WE DIE

Most of us reach the pinnacle of physical strength and athletic ability in our late twenties or early thirties. After that it is downhill. Aging gradually takes its toll. In the United States, 49 percent will develop one or more chronic disease—most commonly diabetes, cancer, heart, or lung disease—accounting for 75 percent of the total cost of healthcare.[18]

> *Forty-nine percent will develop one or more chronic disease.*

People with chronic disease can survive for many years. For others, it becomes clear early in the course of their disease that it will end in death, and the time from the diagnosis varies widely from a few weeks to years. This course can be represented by the following graph.

18. Glen Miller, *Empowering the Patient: How to Reduce the Cost of Healthcare and Improve Its Quality* (Indianapolis: Dog Ear Press, 2009): chapter 4 on chronic diseases.

The following graph shows a typical course for many chronic diseases. After the diagnosis, there will be times when there are sudden exacerbations or complications of the disease represented by the downward blips. With treatment the patient recovers from the acute problem and returns to their usual or reduced level of activity. Repeated complications in many chronic diseases eventually lead to death.

Figure 1: **Advanced life-threatening illness with a steady decline and a short "terminal" phase**[19]

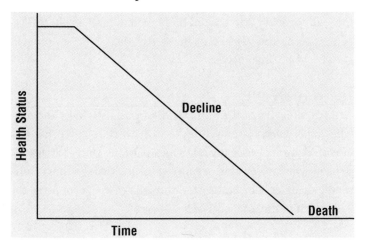

19. http://endlink.lurie.northwestern.edu/index.cfm. *End Link* is an excellent resource for end-of-life care. Their stated purpose: "EndLink was developed as an educational resource for people involved in end-of-life care. Rather than providing answers, we attempt here to offer frameworks for thinking about caring for dying individuals and their families."

Figure 2: **Advanced life-threatening illness marked by slow decline and periodic crises**

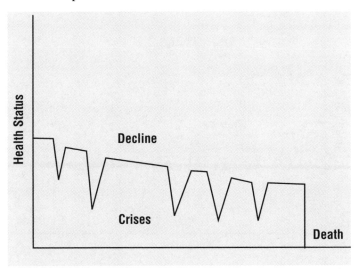

For me this is personal. I am in the dwindling stage of life. I have had health crises: heart attack, a second heart attack, coronary bypass surgery, cardiac arrest, and congestive heart failure. After my first heart attack I confronted the reality of my own death, but that did not translate into any meaningful conversation with Marilyn or other family members and there was no recognition that I was dying. After the second heart attack we did discuss advance directives in a general way; it was only after my cardiac arrest that we seriously began preparing for a good death. Since I first wrote the above words, I had a second cardiac arrest. The defibrillator implanted in my chest wall did what it was designed to do—reestablished an effective blood-pumping heart rhythm. I am still here.

The following graph shows *my* major medical events since my heart attack in 1996. When seen in this perspective, it is clear to me that it is no longer plausible to deny that the inevitable end of my life is death. To deny that is to delay or neglect completing the tasks to enhance the possibility of a good death.

Figure 3: My health status on a time line

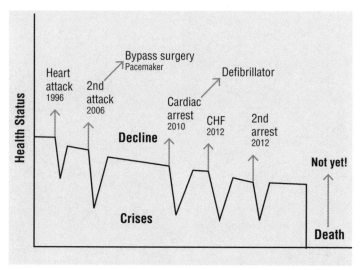

Prior to my cardiac arrest, I hadn't placed any limitations on resuscitation. Given the poor odds of full recovery—including a neurological recovery—and with my abhorrence of a persistently confused state, I now request that there be no CPR performed if my heart stops. As my heart failure progresses, there will be other choices that place limits on my medical care. These are detailed in a later chapter.

QUESTIONS AND SUGGESTIONS FOR DISCUSSION:

1. What does it mean that dying is a "managed process"?

2. Describe the factors in the U.S. healthcare system that promote overtreatment. If you live in Canada, discuss whether the Canadian healthcare system promotes overtreatment.

3. How does "an epidemic of diagnoses" (page 56) affect medical care?

4. What is "defensive medicine" (page 59)?

5. What can the patient do to decrease the doctor's need to practice defensive medicine?

6. At what point in this chapter did the author become aware of his own mortality?

7. What will it take for you to fully recognize that your life will have an end?

Four

Dying Regrets or Loving Memories

[The] capacity to be a family from now on will derive from how you die, not of what but how you did it.
—Steve Jenkinson in *Grief Walker* speaking to a mother with a terminal illness[1]

"**LET ME TELL YOU** about my father," Mayo said to me on a Sunday morning after church. The story of his father's dying time illustrates the difficulty of making decisions when faced with problems associated with advanced age.

My father, Jorge, had a loving family, good health, and a clear mind until he turned ninety and became progressively more confused. At ninety-five, frail and disoriented, he developed an abdominal problem. His doctor recommended an operation to establish a diagnosis. My sister remembered that our father had said, "*Prefiero morir entero que vivir en pedacitos*" (I prefer to die complete rather than to live in little pieces). After discussion, the children didn't allow the exploratory surgery. Jorge recovered from his immediate problem without surgery and died quietly three weeks later.

---

1. *Grief Walker,* a documentary movie by the National Film Board of Canada, written and directed by Tim Wilson, http://www.nfb.ca/film/griefwalker.

Jorge had lost his cognitive ability and was no longer "complete." His children decided against the recommended surgery, recognizing that it would only prolong Jorge's diminished life. In doing this, Jorge's family was opting to allow the natural course of events to occur rather than a painful intervention. For Jorge's family, deciding to forego the surgery was the loving thing to do.

> *For Jorge's family, deciding to forego the surgery was the loving thing to do.*

The decisions about how much and what kind of end-of-life healthcare are not easy. Death is permanent and our instincts tell us that extending life is the only priority. However, in trying to eke out more days, weeks, or months, we may extend suffering and simply prolong a life that has little quality left.

There are other factors that contribute to the difficulty in making these decisions. The family feels that the doctor, with her vast knowledge, certainly must know what's best. Family members can feel insecure and out of place—like being in a foreign land with a hard-to-understand language. Simple things like maneuvering around the cords and tubes attached to their parent add to that feeling.

Frequently, doctors urgently ask for family decisions to know what course to take. So the family, already under the stress of the serious illness of their parent, now must act. In some families decision making will be much more difficult because family members have a history of not communicating well.

So here is the family, intimidated by the hospital and feeling inadequate because of limited knowledge, needing to make life-and-death decisions at a time of tension, stress, and expense. This scenario can be dramatically ameliorated if—as in Jorge's case—the family has their discussion well ahead of any medical crisis.

The first consideration for a family in this situation must be what father (or mother) would want done. Too often, families of elderly patients opt for surgery and life-support measures when quality of life disappeared long ago. The effort to extend life may be only prolonging dying, often at the expense of pro-tracted pain and suffering. The choice for medical interventions may directly oppose the patient's stated wishes.

The lessons from Jorge's story, summarized:

- The first consideration for the family: what would our mother/father want?

- The option to *not do something* always deserves to be considered.

- Family discussions need to take place well before a medical crisis.

- A parent and his or her family need to agree on a spokesperson.

- The family can prepare to ask questions by perusing the Internet and other sources.

MOTHER

The following story, a composite from my decades as a physician caring for elderly patients, could be the story of anyone's mother. This story hones in on the implications of making a choice for or against placing Mother on a breathing machine for her pneumonia. Take note of the significance of Mother's quality of life and the respect for her values in considering what is best for her.

Mother's husband died many years ago, and she's now beginning to show signs of aging with a tottering gait and forgetfulness. As her children consider the possible care options for her, they remember from informal discussions over the past few years that she doesn't think dying is the worst thing that could happen to her. They know that she always dressed carefully, carried herself with dignity, and valued her privacy. She prepared advance directives, placing limits on the medical care she wants, and her children understand and respect those wishes.

As Mother ages and gets feebler, she continues to live in her home but her heart trouble limits her activity and one of her daughters checks on her daily. When she develops a cough and fever, her doctor hospitalizes her for suspected pneumonia.

In the hospital, she has now entered a new arena where a host of often difficult decisions need to be made. Here the doctor is a powerful figure because of superior medical information and knowledge of how to navigate the healthcare system. Mother's life is in danger and family members are understandably tense and emotional.

The hospital attendants replace Mother's clothes with the traditional hospital garb. Her daily routines of the last years are now gone. In her strange surroundings and coupled with fever and breathing difficulties, Mother becomes confused and disoriented. She is unable to make healthcare decisions and her children must make them for her. When Mother's condition worsens further, the doctor meets with the children to recommend transferring her to ICU and placing her on assisted ventilation.

There are several possibilities that are now likely to occur. The children listen carefully to the doctor, and in the stress of needing an immediate decision, they neglect to consider Mother's advance directives. They accept the doctor's advice and she is transferred to the ICU where a tube is placed into her trachea and a ventilator breathes for her. After several days the doctor will try to wean her off the assisted ventilation as he treats her pneumonia. If she continues to require the assisted ventilation, the family will face the heartrending decision of when to stop the machine and allow for the natural course of events to occur.

First and foremost, what would she want?

Prior to being placed on a ventilator, the family needs answers to a number of questions: First and foremost, what would she want? If, after considering her wishes, the family decides in favor of the ICU, other questions need answers: Will she be more comfortable? Can we talk to her? What will be the quality of her life if she survives? How will we know if she is improving? If she is not improving, how long do we continue the ventilator? Who will decide to stop the ventilator if she is not improving? Can we agree to a definite time-limited trial before placing her on the ventilator?

The second possibility is that the children remember that their mother expressed her wishes in anticipation of this kind of situation. They review her advance directives and recall their mother's words that dying is not the worst thing that can happen. The children remember Mother's belief in an afterlife as a place free of pain and suffering. They realize that if she were aware, she would detest the procedures and manipulation that assault her dignity and privacy. After discussion, they agree to provide her with supportive care and antibiotics for her pneumonia but decline the doctor's recommendation for transfer to ICU. They know their mother's life may be shortened but they feel certain they are following her wishes.

PREPARATION FOR A MEDICAL CRISIS

For 85 percent of elderly patients, a family member or another person will make end-of-life healthcare decisions for them. Elderly people and their children need to prepare for this possibility *before* a medical crisis occurs. That preparation will include advance directives fully discussed with their children and reviewed regularly. Since the specifics of a medical crisis are unpredictable, it is imperative that the people making the medical decisions for the elderly patient understand the *spirit* of the directives. That will allow them to more confidently apply the wishes of their loved one to the inevitable variations in any ensuing medical crisis. In the hospital, preparation is essential to know what questions to ask before making decisions about medical care. Various websites list appropriate questions for a wide range of conditions.[2]

PREPARATION STARTS WITH THE FIRST DOCTOR VISIT

It was my first visit to a new cardiologist nearer home. The doctor and staff were competent and communicative. With the records that had been transferred, they clearly had a good grasp of my medical condition. They took vital signs and dutifully checked all the questions on their computerized form. The doctor's exam and conversation were helpful and confidence building. After I returned home I realized what *hadn't happened* on that first visit:

- I wished they had asked me, "How do you see your situation?" or "What are you concerned about for the future?"

- Questions I wished I had asked them:

  - Who do I call for prescription refills?

  - In my condition of congestive heart failure, what do I watch for?

  - What constitutes an emergency and when do I call for help?

  - After an episode of ventricular fibrillation, is there any thing I need to do urgently?

---

2. See appendix 3 for a list.

- Who can I call in case of an emergency on nights and weekends?

- Can we discuss my advance directives?

Remember, I'm a retired doctor, and I forgot to ask these important questions! No question about it—you will improve the quality of your medical care if you prepare before going to the doctor. The appendix has online sources with easy-to-read descriptions of diseases and can prepare you to ask the right questions.

LIFE-EXTENDING MEASURES

The following story illustrates the extent to which medical technology can take on a life of its own despite advance directives and the good intentions of caregivers.

Over her lifetime, Ruth earned the love and respect of her family and many friends by dedicating herself to service and concern for others. She juggled the roles of wife, mother, grandmother, and missionary to Japan for more than three decades. Her family treated her with the deference and accorded her the dignity she deserved.

As retirement approached, Ruth developed persistent and increasingly severe back pain. An operation for suspected narrowing of the spinal canal (spinal stenosis) provided no relief. At seventy-five, she faced spending the rest of her life with unremitting back pain. She consulted a doctor who'd had success in similar cases. After being informed of the risks of the fairly radical surgery, she and her family decided to proceed.

At first it seemed the surgery was a success. "My back doesn't hurt!" Ruth said with joy and amazement after the operation. When her husband, Charley, visited the following morning, though, she was visibly upset and a short time later she went into respiratory failure. With her life in danger, the doctors advised assisted ventilation. They moved her into an intensive care unit, inserted an endotracheal tube (a breathing tube), and connected her to a ventilation machine.

Ruth had previously discussed with her family the amount of healthcare and life-support measures she wanted. She had said clearly that she wanted "no heroic care," which should have ruled out assisted ventilation. The urgency of the situation and the doctor's strong recommendation led the family to accept the assistance, however. She remained in intensive care for eighteen days. During that time, repeated attempts to wean her off her assisted ventilation were unsuccessful. Eventually, her doctors inserted a PICC line (peripherally inserted central catheter) to improve the delivery of intravenous fluids and a feeding tube to supply nutrition. They also performed a tracheostomy—a tube inserted through an incision in her neck in order to keep her connected to the breathing machine. Her request for no heroic care should have excluded all of these procedures.

On the day before she died, Ruth, whose hands were tied to the bed in order to prevent her from pulling out the tubes, wrote an emphatic message to Charley, "Untie my hands now!" When he saw no improvement, Charley called a friend, an experienced ICU nurse, to ask her advice. "She helped me see reality," he said. Along with his family, he decided to end the life-support measures. He told me they felt "they had punished Ruth too much already." Ruth died in the ICU of heart failure eighteen days after her surgery.

The pain of separation caused by a loved one's death is hard, but after Ruth died her family felt the added pain of remorse and self-reproach. The family's final image of Ruth contradicted what they knew and wanted to remember about her. Their desire to provide loving care to their wife and mother took them in in a direction where they lost their chance for loving goodbyes and final words of blessing that might sustain them.

Several years later, reflecting on the experience, Charley said, "The decisions we made were on the best advice available to us. The recommendations of the doctors all seemed reasonable at the time."

> *The recommendations of the doctors all seemed reasonable at the time.*

I can feel the pain and stress of this month-long travail of Charley and his family. There is no way to fully prepare for this. They can take comfort from the fact that it was Ruth's choice to proceed with surgery knowing the risks involved.

A GOOD DEATH

The way Dick died stands in contrast to Ruth's death.

In addition to dignity and privacy, for many of us, control over decisions that affect our own outcomes and shape our future has always been of paramount importance. To give up control is to become a victim of circumstances—a distressing position for anyone.

After Dick was told his diagnosis of lung cancer, he sat under a tree on his property for two hours thinking about what to do with the life he now assumed would be significantly shortened. He decided to sell his business, put his financial affairs in order, and buy a boat. No victim mentality here.

When Dick was thirty, he was out of a job and without the means to support his pregnant wife and two children. The agribusiness company he worked for had folded. Over the next few years, he worked at several odd jobs until he was able to raise the money to buy his former company.

Dick was an excellent manager and sales person and his business became highly successful. Ten years after he started, his accountant informed him that his net assets exceeded one million dollars. He had a direct way of relating to friends and family that engendered trust. He also enjoyed practical jokes, including those pulled on him. I vividly recall how he leaned over a basement railing, laughing about how he had duped his friends into believing he was named "Racquetball Player of the Year." Later, he had to confess his trickery when a friend called his bluff by sending a fake reporter out to interview him.

Everyone deserves to die in a way that reflects the way they lived.

In his early fifties, Dick developed a troubling cough. X-rays and a biopsy confirmed that he had lung cancer. Doctors treated the cancer with radiation and chemotherapy without any promise of a cure. Throughout his two-year illness, Dick retained his sense of humor. When he survived a near-brush with death due to complications from the cancer, he looked at his son Phil and said, "I guess you'll have to wait a while longer to get the Camaro." When telemarketers called, he adopted a monotone voice and said, "I got cancer." He told me, "You would be surprised how fast someone can hang up after that." He also found humor in his chemotherapy-induced baldness.

In time, Dick's disease progressed to the point where he needed repeated blood transfusions and fluid removed from his chest about every three weeks. Finally, he called a halt to any further medical intervention. As a business-person, he was accustomed to making decisions. He seldom second-guessed his decisions and this time was no different. The day came when he informed his family it was time to die. They and his closest friends gathered around him and he said goodbye to each one. Then he closed his eyes, folded his arms, and went into a deep sleep. When he awoke six hours later, he was disappointed he hadn't died. But later that day he did.

The way Dick managed his dying is an inspiration. He didn't succumb to despair after the diagnosis of cancer but remained intentional and purposeful about how he wanted to live the remainder of his life. Even as he sought the best of medical care, he recognized its limitations. And he remained true to himself, retaining his sense of humor and way of relating to others. As his disease progressed, he found new ways of relating. After living with cancer for a year, he said, "If I could make a choice between having cancer or missing what I experienced in the last year, I would take the cancer."

CONCLUSION

The process of dying has changed due to medical technology and life-support devices. There are now more options for treatment that require decisions. As organs fail, decisions about life-extending measures need to take into account the elderly patient's quality of life. This is particularly true in cases of dementia and failing cognitive ability.

Everyone deserves to die in a way that reflects the way they lived, taking into account their values (personal dignity, privacy, and need for control), family issues (caretaker stress, financial cost, and the creation of good memories), and theology (as a source of hope and comfort and views of an afterlife). These and other issues—where to die and specific preparations to die—will be discussed in detail in later chapters.

QUESTIONS AND SUGGESTIONS FOR DISCUSSION:

1. In Mother's story, what are Mother's values that apply to her time of dying?

2. Compare Ruth's and Dick's stories in how their time of dying created loving memories or feelings of remorse for the surviving family.

3. Role-play a situation between a doctor and the adult child of an elderly parent, the consideration of various options, and particularly the option to *not* do something.

4. State in your own words the meaning that "technology can take on a life of its own." Share stories in which you or someone you know experienced that.

Five

Practical Ways to Prepare for a Good Death

*Somebody should tell us, right at the start of our lives that
we are dying. Then we might live life to the limit, every
minute of every day. Do it! I say. Whatever you want to do,
do it now! There are only so many tomorrows.*
—Pope Paul VI[1]

FOR MANY OF US, fear of death is real and we avoid any thoughts about dying. A psychotherapist writing of her personal experience illustrates this death-denying view: "I was preoccupied with thoughts and fears of losing her, and I was very afraid of witnessing her physical deterioration and her death."[2] She was writing about her ninety-nine-year-old mother who was dying of cancer.

People die: suddenly or after an extended illness, with bitterness or gracefully, horrifically or peacefully. But we all die. That fact has been recognized across time and cultures:

We are on a market trip on earth,
Whether we fill our baskets or not,
Once our time is up, we go home. (Igbo song, Nigeria)

---

1. *Brainy Quote,* accessed March 5, 2013, http://www.brainyquote.com/quotes/quotes/p/popepaulvi120383.html.

2. Linda G. Beeler, "Turning a Home into a Hospital," *New York Times,* November 26, 2012.

In the Old Testament, the psalmist says:

"When we look at the wise, they die; fool and dolt perish together" (Psalm 49:10). "Mortals cannot abide in their pomp; they are like the animals that perish" (Psalm 49:12). "The grass withers, the flower fades . . . surely the people are grass" (Isaiah 40:7, all NRSV).

Attitudes toward death differ, from rage—

Welsh poet Dylan Thomas (1914–1953) wrote the famous villanelle that opens with "Do not go gentle into the good night, Old age should burn and rage at close of day; Rage, rage against the dying of the light."[3]

To gentle acceptance—

A gracious lady came to us
and favored us by receiving
kindly our care of her
at the end of all her days.

She was a lady made graceful
beyond what we had known
by the welcome she gave to death,
her guest, whom she made unfearful

by her fearlessness, having no further
use for herself as we had known her.[4]

When I was growing up, family and neighbors spoke of death only in whispers. Even today, we may substitute words

---

3. Excerpted from "Do Not Go Gentle into That Good Night" by Dylan Thomas, accessed March 12, 2013, http://www.poemhunter.com/poem/do-not-go-gentle-into-that-good-night/.

4. Wendell Berry, "VII: Dee Rice Amyx, 1910–2004," *Given: Poems* (Berkley, CA: Counterpoint, 2006). Copyright © 2005 by Wendell Berry from *Given Poems*. Used by permission of Counterpoint.

like *passed on* or *is no more*. If you need to expand your vocabulary of alternate ways to say *dead*, check out the very funny Monty Python skit of the dead parrot.[5] There you will find colorful euphemisms for death like *pining for the fjords, gone to meet its maker, stiff, rest in peace, joined the choir invisible, has rung down the curtain.*

Every year, thousands of elderly patients suffering from chronic disease follow the same pattern. Their disease smolders along for months or years until a crisis strikes. The patient and their families are suddenly thrust into a tense situation with all the emotions that accompany the serious illness of their elderly loved one. They are in denial: *this can't be happening.* They may have had no experience that prepared them for the necessary complicated medical decisions.

What the patient wants can be forgotten or ignored.

The family eagerly waits for news from the doctor who appears all-knowing. The doctor explains the situation and typically needs an immediate decision that may have far-reaching consequences. About 85 percent of the time, the elderly patient will be unable to make the necessary medical decisions. Likely, the family has no trusted source of information to turn to and little time to formulate questions to clarify the issues.

The family wants to "do everything possible," fueled by the natural instinct to postpone death. Other dynamics can come into play, such as guilt because a parent was too-long neglected, or avoidance of potential criticism directed toward the family. In these tense and confusing circumstances, what the patient wants can be forgotten or ignored.

In this situation, it is essential that the family review any advance directives and conversations with the patient that will give direction to how much and what kind of medical care the

5. http://www.youtube.com/watch?v=4vuW6tQ0218.

patient would want. The family needs to be prepared to ask questions and will do well to remember to consider the option of *not* doing a test or intervention. See appendix 3 for a list of sources that will help in understanding the questions to ask.

ADVANCE DIRECTIVES

Advance planning with advance directives is essential to making decisions at the time of a medical crisis. A federal law, the Patient Self-Determination Act, passed in 1991, provides the legal basis for advance directives. All fifty states passed supplemental laws that support its provisions.

In Canada, there have been several province-wide programs to promote advance planning. In 2008 a study process was completed to provide a national framework for advance care plans. Their 2012 report states: "The Advance Care Plan is a written document setting out a person's wishes with respect to medical treatment or personal care, and may include detailed instructions as well as the expressions of the person's values, beliefs, and goals."[6]

Advance directives provide for medical care if the patient is unable to participate in making decisions. Advance planning will make more certain that the patient's medical care is appropriate—decreasing the possibility of over- or under-treatment—and consistent with the patient's wishes. It will reduce stress for the family, remove some of the uncertainty, and lessen feelings of inadequacy. Advance directives will also name a surrogate to make healthcare decisions in the event the patient is unable to do so.

See appendix 3 for excellent sources to guide you in preparing advance directives. Following are guidelines in writing advance directives.

---

6.   Canadian Hospice Palative Care Association, *Advance Care Planning in Canada: National Framework* (January 2012), http://www.advancecareplanning.ca/media/40158/acp%20framework%202012%20eng.pdf.

1. Do the advance directives (AD) well in advance of a medical crisis.

2. In consultation with your family, establish who will serve as power of attorney for health care decisions (PAHCD) or power of attorney for personal care in Canada.

3. Be clear about any limitations on medical interventions such as CPR, assisted ventilation, and tube feedings (see a more complete listing of possible limitations on page 85).

4. Take the time to openly and thoroughly discuss your wishes with your children and any other significant family/friends/relatives.

5. Make certain the living will (LW) and AD are properly signed.

6. Give copies of these documents to your PAHCD, the hospital, your doctor, pastor, and attorney.

7. Review the AD with family members at least once per year and *at the time of any medical crisis.*

8. At the time of a medical crisis, inform the doctor of the provisions of your AD and your expectations that the provisions of the LW and AD will be respected.

Five Wishes,[7] an online resource, is an expanded way of expressing advance directives. Dr. Douglas Smucker, palliative care physician said, "I have found *Five Wishes* to be very useful for people without a medical background. Written in plain language, it asks the question 'what do I want done in different medical circumstances?'" Persons who use this method have found it to be helpful in sorting through the options for medical care for their loved one. *Five Wishes* provides an easy-to-

---

7. Aging with Dignity, www.agingwithdignity.org.

understand form that can be filled out, placed on file, and can be made available to healthcare providers. Parents who clearly define their desires for end-of-life healthcare are giving a real gift to their children.

HOW DOCTORS DIE

Of course, even doctors die; no one needs to tell any of us that. Dr. Ken Murray, a physician, wrote a pertinent article, "How Doctors Die," giving insight into how doctors think about this topic:[8]

> *Doctors know the futility of medical procedures in the dying patient.*

Of course, doctors don't want to die; they want to live. But they know enough about modern medicine to know its limits. And they know enough about death to know what all people fear most: dying in pain, and dying alone. They want to be sure, when the time comes, that no heroic measures will happen. . . . Almost all medical professionals have seen what we call "futile care" being performed on people. That's when doctors bring the cutting edge of technology to bear on a grievously ill person near the end of life. The patient will get cut open, perforated with tubes, hooked up to machines, and assaulted with drugs.

Doctors know the futility of medical procedures in the dying patient. A large group of doctors were asked what they want done if they have irreversible brain damage.[9] These

---

8. Ken Murray, MD, "How Doctors Die: It's Not Like the Rest of Us, But It Should Be," *Zocalo, Public Square* (November 30, 2011), http://www.zocalopublicsquare.org/2011/11/30/how-doctors-die/ideas/nexus/.

9. Casey Chan, "Doctors Don't Follow Their Own Advice on Medical Treatment," *Medical Science* (January 18, 2013), http://gizmodo.com/5976978/doctors-dont-want-treatment-even-when-theyre-dying.

doctors were nearly unanimous in rejecting most of these interventions:

Percent of doctors rejecting medical interventions if they have irreversible brain damage:

Cardiopulmonary resuscitation (CPR)	92%
Mechanical ventilation	90%
Feeding tube	77%
Major surgery	87%
Dialysis	89%
Chemotherapy for cancer	88%
Invasive diagnostic procedures	83%
Transfusions of blood or blood products	82%
Antibiotics	75%

Most doctors rejected the use of these nine medical interventions if afflicted with irreversible brain damage. I am in full agreement with the doctors in the survey. For me, irreversible brain damage and the attendant disorientation and confusion are worse than death. If I am in a permanently confused or unresponsive state, I see no point in intervening in ways that will only prolong my dying.

DNR ORDER

Most hospitals and nursing homes ask their patients upon admission whether they want the order "Do not resuscitate" (DNR) placed on their chart. DNR is the patient's stated wish that if his or her heart or breathing stops, there will be no interventions to restart the heartbeat or breathing. There are situations where patients don't want to be resuscitated. A standing DNR can then be recorded in advance directives and communicated to the doctor. A doctor's DNR order written in the hospital or nursing home instructs nurses and other caretakers that there is to be no CPR.

A sudden cardiac arrest is usually due to ventricular fibrillation or ventricular tachycardia—short-circuited electrical activity—that causes the heart to lose its ability to pump blood. An electrical shock is necessary to convert the heart to a functional rhythm. If a defibrillator is not readily available, CPR is done by rapid manual chest compressions. If the CPR is prolonged, a tube may be placed into the trachea to maintain breathing. The chance of survival decreases 10 to 15 percent for each minute of delay in starting effective CPR.

The American Heart Association states that EMT units treat about three hundred thousand cases of cardiac arrest each year. There are thousands of persons still alive and fully functional who have survived a cardiac arrest because of CPR. I am one of these people. The chance of survival after a cardiac arrest and CPR decreases with age. The survival rate for patients in their forties and fifties is 10 percent, 8.1 percent in their sixties, 7.1 percent in their seventies, and 3.3 percent after the age of eighty.[10]

There are significant complications to CPR including broken ribs, collapsed lungs, and subsequent organ failure. Tragically, for some persons, the heart rhythm is restored but there is permanent brain damage because of the lack of oxygen for a critical period. The family can then face weeks, months, or years with a loved one who exists in body but has little or no ability to relate.

A DNR order is not a death wish.

A DNR order is not a death wish. A DNR order allows natural events such as sudden cardiac rhythm problems or other organ failure to end the life without the intervention of CPR. Patients considering a DNR order need to take into account the stage and curability of their disease, their quality of life, and the success rates and complications of CPR.

10. Paula Span, "How Successful Is CPR in Older Patients?" *New York Times*, August 9, 2012, http://newoldage.blogs.nytimes.com/2012/08/09/how-successful-is-cpr-in-older-patients/.

When the legs fill with the fluid of heart failure, when the BUN (blood urea nitrogen) rises because the kidneys no longer filter out the blood impurities, when the breath becomes short on minimal exertion, when the doctors say there is nothing more to do for the cancer, it is time to recognize the inevitable—you are dying. This is the time to consider if you want to be resuscitated in the event that your heart stops beating.

When to consider a DNR order:

- All medical resources were explored and considered. The best of medical care says that further treatment would be futile or the treatment has become onerous beyond the tolerance of the patient.

- Cancer is no longer responding to treatment.

- Progressive organ failure (such as heart, kidney, liver, lung)

- Progressive dementia or persistent coma

- Intolerable and uncontrollable pain

- Before risky surgery (Note, however, that many surgeons will not do surgery with a DNR order in place.)

- Incapacitation of any other origin

MY DECISION ON DNR AND PACEMAKER

I have been there. I was resuscitated and recovered my pre-arrest status. I was no smarter after my arrest, but I did have my wits and was able to function as before.

However, having been through the experience with the realization that I had beaten the odds and knowing the slim chance of recovery—or worse, physical recovery with the loss of cognitive ability—I don't want to take the chance again. I have decided in favor of DNR and no CPR in the event of another cardiac arrest.

In October 2010, I agreed to an ICD (implantable cardiac device). The ICD is a pacemaker and a defibrillator about the size of a flattened tangerine implanted under the skin below my left clavicle. On December 27, 2012, the ICD proved its worth when it fired off and converted my ventricular fibrillation to a functional rhythm. I wouldn't be here otherwise to tell the story. Once again, I am thankful for the technology that kept me walking the earth. However, I foresee the possibility of a change in my situation when I will request that my ICD be deactivated and the natural course of events determine my end.

Therefore, in the event that I am *unable to speak for myself*, under the following conditions I request that my durable power of attorney for health decisions notify my medical caregivers to deactivate my defibrillator:

- When a DNR order is in effect for any reason

- Diagnosis of Alzheimer's disease or progressive dementia of any sort

- Debilitating condition such as a stroke

- Intractable and severe pain

- Diagnosis of progressive cancer

- Progressive organ failure such as kidney or heart failure

- Any situation where I am approaching the end of my life

By taking this step, I recognize that I may live for months or years with the defibrillator turned off but in the event of a fatal heart rhythm, the defibrillator will not fire off and I will die a natural death.

Further, in the above situations, if it becomes apparent that my pacemaker is prolonging my dying, I request that it also be turned off. Medical ethicists agree that deactivation of a pacemaker is ethical, summed up by their statement that "there is no ethical or legal distinction between withholding a pacemaker and deactivating one after it has been initiated." [11]

SPECIFIC PREPARATION

Am I dying? The answer must be yes. My heart is weakened by two heart attacks. One of my medical diagnoses is "congestive heart failure." I have had two cardiac arrests and face the possibility of more. Barring an accident or other catastrophic disease, I know what my terminal disease is—congestive heart failure.

It is time to recognize my state of health for what it is.

It is no longer plausible to deny the inevitable. It is time to recognize my state of health for what it is and make plans to try to ensure a more orderly process of dying, to enhance the possibility of retaining some control of the process, and to prepare the family. I discussed and made advance plans with my family for the time of crisis.

- My wife, Marilyn, and I discussed her response if I don't wake up from a nap. In the state of Indiana, unless I am under the care of hospice, she will call 911. The EMT squad will respond, prepared to start CPR. If it is determined that I am dead-dead, beyond the possibility of reviving with CPR, the police will need to decide if I died of natural causes and then report to the coroner. Only then can the funeral home be called to pick up the "remains" (a curious word indeed).

- We (Marilyn and I) met with our son and daughter, the two executors of our estate and power of attorney for healthcare decisions (PAHCD). I went prepared with information on

---

11. Parag Bharadwaj, MD, and Katherine T. Ward, MD, "Ethical Considerations of Patients with Pacemakers," *American Family Physician* 78, no. 3 (August 1, 2008):398–99, http://www.aafp.org/afp/2008/0801/p398.html.

our banking account including online access with the user ID and passwords. I gave them information that indicated the automatic payments from the banking account and the direct deposits into the account.

- We reviewed our advance directives (again) and talked about specific situations and how they may play out. We emphasized that there will likely be situations that don't permit easy classification and encouraged them to use their best judgment in carrying out the spirit of our wishes for end-of-life care.

- We showed them where they will find the original copy of our will, living will, durable power of attorney for health decisions, and advance directives. (Each of them already had copies of these documents.)

- We discussed our desire to die at home unless the medical care requires hospitalization or the necessary care is too taxing for the family.

- We discussed our advance plans for our funerals, stating our preferences regarding memorial services and public viewing.

These discussions with Marilyn and two of our children were in a calm and unhurried atmosphere without the emotion attendant to a medical crisis. There was time to explore subtle meanings of words that gave me assurance that they understood my intentions. As a result of these preparations and the meeting with my children acting as my PAHCDs, I am confident that decisions they make on my behalf will accurately reflect my wishes.

HEALTHCARE ADVOCATE

To ask someone to represent and speak for us requires a high level of trust. A trusting, comfortable relationship does not just happen. It needs to be worked at. People in their declining years need to make it a priority to cultivate their relationship with their spouse, child, or other person chosen to speak for them.

Your advocate will be the same person that you name as your durable power of attorney for healthcare decisions. This person, in addition to his or her relationship with you, ideally needs a working knowledge of how to navigate the healthcare system and an understanding of privacy and confidentiality issues. It is essential that the advocate have the confidence of and good communication with other family members.

*A high level of trust is necessary
to be a healthcare advocate.*

Ruth, an experienced ICU nurse, became an advocate for her patient in the following story:

Last week I admitted an eighty-year-old woman who was in her last stages of COPD (chronic obstructive pulmonary disease) and lung cancer. She developed pneumonia and was admitted to the hospital because of progressive respiratory failure. She had completed a living will with her family stating that she would never want to have a tube in her windpipe and be hooked to a breathing machine. On this admission, the doctor and family agreed to antibiotics for her pneumonia, but should she arrest—either cardiac or respiratory—we would not intervene with CPR or assisted ventilation.

Several days after admission, her condition worsened and she was much weaker. Her physician asked her if she would be willing to have a tube put down her airway temporarily to give her a few days of rest. He said, "If this doesn't work we can stop the treatment." The patient nodded weakly in agreement and she was transferred to the ICU.

After arriving in ICU, I [Ruth] learned that the family had a lot of reservations about the decision to place her on assisted ventilation and how the decision was made. They were distressed because she had "agreed" to the tube and yet they knew she didn't want that.

I felt I needed to be an advocate for the patient and the family. We talked about the reason for living wills—to make decisions *before* a medical crisis when the patient is coherent and able to participate in the discussion. I explained to them what was involved in placing a tube in the trachea, including sedation, arm and leg restraints, and inability to talk or eat. I also explained that given her history of end stage COPD and her age, it was highly unlikely that she could be weaned off the ventilator. They soon decided that they wanted to honor her initial wish not to insert the tube.

I called in the ICU physician who was comfortable with their decision. The patient was transferred out of ICU to a palliative care floor. The doctor wrote orders for DNR and to keep her comfortable. She died peacefully the next day with her family at the bedside.

I was appalled that the physician had asked the patient to change her code status when she was drowsy, short of breath, and communicated only with a nod or shake of her head. This had been a well-thought-out decision made by the patient and family well before the crisis. At that point, a living will comes into play and the physician should have talked to the daughter, not the patient."

Ruth felt what other nurses feel, that *too much care* is being given to dying patients. Theresa Brown[12] describes her feel-

---

12. Theresa Brown, RN, "Prolonging Death at the End of Life," *New York Times,* September 9, 2009, http://well.blogs.nytimes.com/2009/09/09/prolonging-death-at-the-end-of-life/.

ings as a nurse providing continued aggressive care to a patient when further treatment was clearly futile. She names this concern as "moral distress," defined as "the anxiety, fatigue and hopelessness that providers experience in the face of medically futile care." Brown states: "It's estimated that as many as 15 to 25 percent of nurses quit their jobs as a result of moral distress, also never to return."

LOSS OF CONTROL: ON A CONVEYOR BELT

Most people throughout their lifetime have been accustomed to having a sense of control over events. Frustration, confusion, and anxiety ensue when events seem to be spiraling out of control. Things were happening too fast for Helen, newly diagnosed with cancer. When she called me to talk, we set a time and I suggested she put the coffeepot on, letting her know this meeting would not be rushed.

> *"I feel that I am on a conveyer belt and not given the time to make decisions."*

Helen described her progressive symptoms and the consultation with a doctor that led to a scan with a biopsy. Two days later the diagnosis of cancer was confirmed. The following day, she spent three hours listening to the chemotherapist and cancer center social worker describe what was going to happen. On the way out of the hospital, she was given a paper with an appointment two days later for two more scans and plans to place the IV ports on the following Monday. In five days, Helen had a scan, surgical biopsy, extended appointments with the chemotherapist and a cancer social worker, and two more scans. She said, "I am eighty-four years old. I haven't had a chance to catch my breath. I don't know if someone my age should go through the chemotherapy or not. Mostly I feel that

I am on a conveyer belt and not given the time to make decisions."

Helen had earlier set advance directives and had discussed them with her children. All her life she had been deliberate and intentional in making decisions. Now she was being asked to make a major decision without time to think about it or to consider any options. She sensed that she had lost control.

Repeatedly, patients describe their encounter with the healthcare system as "being on a conveyor belt." Implicit in that description is the feeling that things are rushing by too fast without time for adequate discussion and asking what it means. This is when you call time-out, take a deep breath, and give yourself the space to more fully understand the next steps.

There are many well-documented hazards to hospitalization that affect *all* patients. Time and space do not permit a full discussion of this here. There are specific *additional* risks for elderly patients. Delirium is one.

It is essential to find the underlying cause of delirium.

Each year, 20 percent of the 11.8 million elderly patients in this country will develop delirium—different from dementia—defined as the sudden onset of confusion and disorientation that is usually reversible.[13] There are many causes of delirium. It is of utmost importance that the underlying cause is discovered and corrected, which invariably restores the person to his or her normal mental capacity. Some of the inciting causes of delirium are fever, medications, infections, dehydration with electrolyte imbalance, and a variety of endocrine disorders. Medication is a particularly prevalent culprit. One of my roles

---

13. Marcia O. Miller, MD, "Evaluation and Management of Delirium in Hospitalized Older Patients," *Am Fam Physician* 78, no. 11 (December 1, 2008):1265–70, http://www.aafp.org/afp/2008/1201/p1265.html.

as a consulting physician was to take patients *off* their medicines when they presented with the puzzling and sudden onset of delirium.

For the elderly, the dislocation inherent in a hospitalization in conjunction with their illness can cause delirium. Delirium will occur in a high percentage of elderly patients in ICU on assisted ventilation or who undergo surgery.[14] For family members the confusion and disorientation of their parent can be very distressing. It is wise to remember that if the patient's condition improves, the delirium will disappear.

In addition to delirium, Judith Graham in her *New York Times* article[15] cites a number of studies that indicate that for the elderly patient there is significant cognitive impairment both in the hospital and after returning home. Graham points to a study of more than 1,300 patients that showed the rate of cognitive decline doubled for those patients over sixty-five who had been hospitalized.

Dementia, as opposed to delirium, is the gradual onset of disorientation and confusion. Dementia is chronic, progressive, and usually not reversible. The causes of dementia include Alzheimer's disease; brain injury from trauma, strokes, infection, lack of oxygen, or alcohol; and a variety of inherited diseases such as Huntington's disease or Tay-Sachs disease. The incidence of dementia is predicted to increase dramatically in the next fifty years.

DYING AT HOME

In addition to the mental health aspects, there are other clear advantages to dying at home in a familiar setting. Dying at

14. Susan Seliger, "Another Hospital Hazard for the Elderly," *New York Times*, November 2, 2011, http://newoldage.blogs.nytimes.com/2011/11/02/another-hospital-hazard-for-the-elderly/.

15. Judith Graham, "After Hospitalization, Mental Trouble for Elderly Patients," *New York Times*, March 23, 2012, http://newoldage.blogs.nytimes.com/2012/03/23after-hospitalization-mental-trouble-for-elderly-patients/.

home becomes a family affair with the ability to make decisions together in a familiar atmosphere, a sense of control over the proceedings, and sensitivity to the privacy needs of the patient. With the patient's last days in the home, the family can create lasting and loving memories not possible in the hospital.

> *Dying at home becomes a family affair.*

The advantages of dying at home also extend to the care-givers. Studies show that the incidence of prolonged grief and PTSD among caregivers is markedly less when the patient dies at home compared to death in the hospital.[16] Not insignificantly, nor surprisingly, the cost is vastly reduced when death occurs at home.

QUESTIONS AND SUGGESTIONS FOR DISCUSSION:

1. To what extent are dying and death considered a natural part of life in your community? To what extent do you observe people in denial about death?

2. Compare and discuss the way funerals are handled in your community.

3. State in one or two sentences the purpose of advance directives.

4. What are the desirable qualities of the person you designate as your power of attorney for healthcare decisions (PAHCD)?

5. Under what circumstances (if any) would you want a DNR order?

6. Discuss the advantages and disadvantages of dying at home.

---

16. Linda Searing, "Study: Dying at Home May Be Less Traumatic for Patients as Well as Their Caregivers," *The Washington Post,* September 27, 2010, http://www.washingtonpost.com/wp-dyn/content/article/2010/09/27/AR2010092705374.html.

Six

Leaning Forward as Death Approaches

*We all know we're going to die; what's important is
the kind of men and women we are in the face of this.*
—Anne Lamott, *Bird by Bird: Some Instructions
on Writing and Life*

MY FIRST MEDICAL APPOINTMENT of the day was
with Harvey who at sixty-seven had arthritic joints and a failing
heart. I went through the routine of a review of his symptoms,
a physical examination, and an adjustment of his medicines.
He asked me, his physician, what he could expect in the future.
I replied that he could reasonably expect years of life and over
time his arthritis and the weakness of his heart would gradually
further decrease his mobility and endurance. He thought for a
moment and I recall his sadness as he said, "All my life I wanted
to travel to places like Greece and Egypt. Now I know that I will
never be able to do that. I waited too long."

Many elderly people, when asked what they would do if
they had their lives to live over, reply that they would take more
risks, pursue relationships at deeper levels, and find ways to
express their creative side. Oliver Wendell Holmes is reported
to have said, "Most of us go to our graves with our music still
inside us."

Marilyn and I decided we wanted to release the "music still inside us." At age fifty-nine, I left medical practice and we went to India as volunteers to work with a team of Indians to bring a better life to the people there. This made no sense to my medical colleagues who pointed out that my prestige and income were at their peak. But in those seven years in India, our horizons expanded in so many ways: we experienced true hospitality, learned the joy of small successes, and took great pleasure in deep relationships with people of a vastly different culture. At the end of each week, we had the satisfying feeling that we were making a difference. We felt alive and invigorated.

More than twenty years later, I continue to feel the need to be involved and to get on with what I can yet do. On the occasion of our fifty-sixth wedding anniversary, I wrote the following poem for Marilyn.

Gettin' Ready to Live

> All those moments and hours and days
> morphed into years
> when we were gettin' ready to live.

We learned, we trained,
we taught, we modeled,
gettin' ready to live.

> After decades of gettin' ready,
> it is time to start living
> in the moments that make up a life.

To stop gettin' ready and start living.
The prospect enchants and daunts:
what does it mean?

> Living (it seems to me)
> is so related to love

deeply felt and expressed.
Love that finds expression
in the moments of our lives.

Expression, that's the key.
To move past the point of love assumed
with love that acts
and nothing left unsaid. [1]

NOTHING LEFT UNSAID

After I saw the movie *The King's Speech,* I realized that I had something unsaid that I needed to say to my brother Bob, fourteen months older than me.

When Bob was nine years old, our mother lay near death in the hospital after the difficult birth of our youngest brother. Our father was spending most of his time in the hospital over a period of weeks. Uncle Lloyd told Bob, the oldest son, "You are now the man of the house."

Shortly thereafter, Bob began to stutter. As in *The King's Speech,* various treatments were suggested for the stuttering. Bob became adept at saying "Peter Piper picked a peck of pickled peppers" but found he just couldn't work that phrase into everyday conversation. The local chiropractor was said to have treatment for stuttering. I accompanied Bob and my mother to the chiropractor's office. I watched with great interest as he lay Bob face down on the examining table. The chiropractor pushed his fingers deeply into the back of Bob's neck. He gave a sudden twist accompanied by a loud and

---

1. December 18, 2011. This was my first effort at writing poetry. With tongue in cheek, I asked noted author Kathleen Norris what changes I needed to make in my lifestyle now that I am a poet. Without hesitation she answered, "You need to grow a ponytail, wear a French beret, drink espresso coffee, smoke cheroots, and hang out." I decided to work on the hang-out part of Kathleen's prescription.

startling *crack*. That was the end of the treatment. Bob got up off the table and said, "Th-th-that hurt." Clearly there had been no sudden miraculous cure. I recall hoping that the effect of the treatment was still to come.

> Stuttering continued to be a millstone around Bob's neck. I recall sitting next to him as a teenager in a Sunday school class. When the teacher asked each person to read a Bible verse, Bob whispered to me, "Skip me." I read the next Bible verse out of turn, sparing Bob yet another embarrassment. At age eighty-one, he still remembers his feelings when his peers snickered and mimicked him.

> Back to *The King's Speech*. In this film, the king's therapist says to King George VI, "You are the most courageous man I know." The moment I heard that, I realized that I needed to talk to Bob. I told him how much I admire him for the courage it took for him to face the humiliation on a daily basis as he tried to express himself in even the most ordinary conversation. Bob told me—something I had never heard before—that it was only his ability to sing that saved his self-esteem.

Was it essential in the eternal scheme of things to have that talk with Bob? I don't know, but I do know that our relationship is different since. And I feel that I cleared up a bit of history with my brother.

LEANING FORWARD

In the following story, Linea, after her diagnosis of cancer, plunged into activities that had defined her all her adult life. Her acceptance of the reality of death permitted her to *lean forward*, meeting the remaining months head on with grace and gratefulness.

Linea was seventy-three years old when she was diagnosed with advanced cancer[2] that had already spread to her liver, pancreas, and lungs. As a seminary graduate, she had served her church as elder, teacher, and with a team of persons who visited women in jail. She counseled many people in their times of stress.

At the time of diagnosis, her doctors presented three options: to do nothing, to pursue aggressive chemotherapy, or to enter a medical research program. Linea asked questions regarding the chances of improvement, prolongation of life, and sickness induced by the treatment. She opted for the research program after learning that the chemotherapy would cause significant sickness with no real chance of improvement in the cancer. Entering the research program required repeated follow-up studies including blood tests and scans. The doctors estimated that her life expectancy was about six months.

Linea and her husband, Lenny, had worked on their advance directives two years earlier after the tragic accidental death of their son-in-law. They discussed their directives with their children well before the diagnosis of cancer and with repeat discussions annually. Copies of the advance directives were sent to the doctors, hospital, pastor, and their children.

Linea, a gifted writer, accepted the certainty of death and had written many years before:

---

2. The improving survival rates from cancer must be noted. "The number of people with a history of cancer in the United States has increased dramatically, from 3 million in 1971 to about 13.7 million today. About 68% of today's cancer survivors were diagnosed with cancer five or more years ago. And, approximately 15% of all cancer survivors were diagnosed 20 or more years ago. More than half (59%) of cancer survivors are 65 or older, and 5% are younger than 40." http://www.cancer.netsurvivorship/about-survivorship (accessed April 30, 2013).

Creator God,
we are slow fruit on the tree.
Cup us gently,
patient for the moment
when the elements
mature us to sweetness
and you pluck us
for your table.

Linea announced to her church community and other friends that she had cancer. This open communication allowed for expressions of concern. Over the last months of her life, she reported her status each week to her large group of friends.

> *"I am not dying from cancer,
> but living with cancer."*

Friends who want to be helpful would do well to observe a few guidelines in relating to someone with a terminal illness. Ask how the person is doing but not so often that it becomes tedious; call before you visit, and limit your visit to fifteen to twenty minutes.

While Linea had long accepted that death was inevitable, its arrival now became imminent. Her approach to living out those last months was shaped by her statement that "I am not dying *from* cancer, but living *with* cancer."

In these months she made plans for her funeral, memorial service, and the decision to be cremated. She actively downsized her possessions giving books and mementos to family and friends. Jewelry and dishes were apportioned out to specific people who would have a special connection or appreciation for that item. Leftover clothing was given to a thrift store. She taught Lenny some of the rudiments of cooking. They had weekly dinners with a small group of close friends. (Lenny continued this practice after Linea died.)

Linea entered the hospice program with home visits from hospice nurses twice weekly. Eventually, her care required that she be hospitalized. She remained alert and oriented. While in the hospital she was anointed in the Mennonite tradition for "strength and peace in her last days." As her organs began to fail and she became more jaundiced, her family and close friends came and in turn each one said goodbye with hugs and kisses.

Linea came to her time of trial having settled her thoughts about life and the inevitability of death. She had run the race and finished the course, and had done it all with patience for the progressive limitations. She exhibited grace in her continued concern for others with an unfailing experience of a loving God.

In her last months she wrote "To the Death Angel":

Gather me in
While the night rests on morning
Fold me in feathers, in flowers
And swoop and spiral and twirl
With delight at your harvest
Your giant shape on the wall
Is a call I will answer
Your eyes of such burning
Pull rose from my lips
And I come at your bidding
Ready for Eden
Death Angel, I come

—Linea Reimer Geiser

Linea's story illustrates the "opportunity" that came after her diagnosis of cancer to plan for an orderly exit from this life. It all started with her acceptance of death as a reality, which allowed her to devote time to the things that had always mattered to her. When she said, "I am not dying *from* cancer but living *with* cancer," she was saying that she is not defined by her disease—she is much more than her cancer.

The way that Linea lived out her remaining months of life can be a lesson for all of us. She explored the options for treatment with appropriate questions. She had advance directives in place and accepted with equanimity the reality of death. After her diagnosis, she did not withdraw in despair but stayed in close touch with her friends and relatives, welcoming the comfort of her faith community through their visits and eventually with the rite of anointing.

TIME TO REFLECT

The philosopher Socrates said that a life without reflection is not worth living. Reflection on what it all means is essential throughout one's lifespan. The time to reflect is doubly important when any further treatment for cancer is futile, when the heart is failing, or when treatment becomes unbearably onerous. For it is no longer possible to evade the fact that the days remaining are numbered. There will be an end. This is the time to sit and reflect:

- Am I where I want to be? In a place I feel I belong—spiritually, physically, emotionally?

- Am I near people I love?

- Is there opportunity to be involved on a daily basis in things that contribute to others?

- Are there important things that need to be said to specific people?

- And most importantly, who am I and how do I want to live the rest of my life in a way that reflects who I really am?

This is the time for the conversation where members of the family talk openly and freely about end-of-life desires and limitations. The Conversation Project can help: it's a public campaign to "get everyone's end-of-life wishes expressed and respected."[3] The website offers a starter kit to guide you through the conversation that can make the difference between a good death and a bad death.

This is also the time to think about what I am leaving behind. Specifically, what do I want my children and grand-children to remember about me? This can be done by writing an ethical will—different from a financial will or a living will.

Life without reflection is not worth living.

An ethical will[4,5] is an effective way to communicate to your children and grandchildren your values, milestones, and guide-posts along the way, and your wishes for them. This is the place to say how you lived your life, reflect on significant events, and tell a few stories that shaped your life. Author and medical doc-tor Ira Byock stresses that there are four statements that need to be covered: Please forgive me; I forgive you; Thank you; and I love you.[6] Dr. Douglas Smucker, a palliative care doctor I men-tioned earlier, noted the special meaning for family members to read such a statement signed by their loved one after she or he has passed on.

---

3. http://theconversationproject.org/.

4. Barry K. Baines, *Ethical Wills: Putting Your Values on Paper,* 2nd edi-tion (Cambridge, MA: Da Capo Press, 2006).

5. Celebrations of Life, "Ethical Wills/Legacy Letters," http://celebra-tionsoflife.net/ethicalwills/.

6. Ira Byock, MD, *The Four Things That Matter Most: A Book about Living* (New York: Free Press, 2004).

So there is need for action in the time remaining. We have a choice. We can be active, leaning forward to make this the most significant time of our lives—the capstone on a lifetime of experience and relationships—or we can withdraw in self-pity and despair.

> *We have a choice. We can be active or we can withdraw in self-pity and despair.*

What Joan Chittister, author of *The Gift of Years*, says about older people generally applies here.

The truth is that old people tend to come in two flavors— the sour ones and the serene ones. The sour ones are angry at the world for dismissing them from the rank and file of those who run it and control it and own it and are not old in it. They demand that the rest of the world seek them out, pity them, take their orders, stay captive to their scowls.

The serene ones live with soft smiles on their aging faces, a welcome sign to the world of what it means to grow old gracefully.[7]

> *I want to be remembered for a welcoming smile, an attentive ear, and words of encouragement.*

Like Linea, I don't want to be defined by my heart trouble. I am not my heart troubles. I am still a lively being with hopes and aspirations, a sense of humor, trivial and deep thoughts; an individual seeking to learn and remain engaged. I can get up each morning with the attitude that my life has meaning, that I have something to contribute to others, that there are deeper spiritual depths to plumb, and that I still have time and space for growth and new understanding.

---

7. Joan Chittister, *The Gift of Years: Growing Older Gracefully* (New York: BlueBridge, 2008), 39.

As I head for my final exit, I want to be remembered for a welcoming smile, an attentive ear, and words of encouragement. People who visited my brother Virgil to encourage him in his last weeks of life repeatedly said that *their* spirits had been lifted. In preparing for that time, I am making the effort to change from *hurry, hurry* to relaxed times for quiet conversation, from accumulating to divesting, from striving to succeed to reflection on a life well lived, from judging to accepting, and from doing to being.

As death approaches, it is time to re-examine one's relationship with God.

I expect that the biggest adjustment for me will be to change my self-image as a caregiver to a passive recipient. I spent my life as husband, father, grandfather, doctor, medical administrator, and overseas development organizer working to try to make a better life for those I served. That's who I am. So the prospect of the metamorphosis from caregiver into a recipient of care, I view with foreboding. Yet the time will likely come.

My outlook on life has always been steadfastly optimistic—an optimism that was rooted in my mother's attitude. She birthed nine children in thirteen years in the midst of the Great Depression. Over that span, she was pregnant half of the time (81 of 161 months)! She had no maids, no disposable diapers, no automatic washer or dryer, and no shortcuts to meal preparation. What she did have was a chronic scarcity of money. Through it all, mother's attitude was indelibly imprinted on her children that no matter how bad things are today, they will be better tomorrow. That optimism was firmly grounded in her faith in a loving and caring God.

As death approaches, as thoughts turn to the life that is to come, it is time to reexamine one's relationship with God. Pastor Gary's question to his father—himself a pastor—was,

"Are you at peace with God; is there some hidden agenda that you have kept buried in your soul and mind?" (This story is told in more detail in chapter eight.)

That same question faces each of us in our living and in the time of our dying: "Am I at peace with God?" Rob Moll, in his book *The Art of Dying: Living Fully into the Life to Come*,[8] quotes Marge Schaffer: "Dying well . . . means being at peace with God and with the people in your life."

OUR LAST VISIT WITH MERV

Marilyn and I had the rare privilege of being present when Merv, Marilyn's brother, made his peace with God.

Merv is dying. He is Marilyn's brother, younger by four years. He had lived with his cancer for seventeen years. Now for inscrutable reasons the cancer returned with a ferocity that took over his life. When he was informed of the diagnosis and that no treatment was available, Merv described a time of panic and utter despair that lasted for three miserable hours. He now understood that the cancer was his terminal disease. He accepted the diagnosis and its inevitable end.

We freely discussed his condition and expectations for the future. I assured him that there will be medicines that will control pain when and if needed. We corrected their impression that hospice care was available only in the last few days of life and urged them to contact this service.

We saw Merv again several weeks later, one week before he took to his bed and never got up again. His condition had deteriorated in the three weeks since we had seen him. Fat and muscle appeared to have melted away from his bones and week-long facial hair covered his gaunt face. Despite his

---

8. Rob Moll, *The Art of Dying: Living Fully into the Life to Come* (Downers Grove, IL: InterVarsity Press, 2010).

obvious decline, Merv's mind was entirely clear. We talked about how he was feeling and the evidence that the cancer was progressing.

I had been in the presence of many dying patients, but this was different. I went to his bedside as a brother-in-law and soon found myself in the role of a pastor. I asked this church-going Lutheran if he would welcome prayer. He indicated he would.

Marilyn read the twenty-third psalm. With Marilyn and myself on opposite sides of the bed holding Merv's hands, I started my prayer by saying, "God, this is Merv. He is coming to you soon." I went on to say that Merv is not a perfect human being and is presenting himself with his faults and imperfections. I expressed confidence that Jesus will be with him to escort him through the "valley of the shadow of death." I expressed assurance that the same God who created him will receive him back into the divine loving presence.

Merv remained fully aware. He lay with his eyes closed and then he began to pray, thanking God for a good life and for Norma, his wife heroically caring for him, and then confessing his failures and imperfections. Despite his condition and sedating medication, he remained focused on what he wanted to say. He opened his eyes, looked at Marilyn and said, "You have been a good sister." Both of us kissed him, wished him God's blessing, and said goodbye, knowing this was the final parting. His facial expression and relaxed body assured us that Merv was at peace. He died peacefully three weeks later in the care of hospice.

I recall that in my growing-up years at the time of communion in our Mennonite church, the bishop asked church members, "Are you at peace with God and your neighbors?" In our family and community living at peace with God and other persons was the consciously strived-for way of life. The question returns forcefully at the end of life. For Christians, the ability to answer that question in the affirmative with quiet confidence is an important part of a good death.

QUESTIONS AND SUGGESTIONS FOR DISCUSSION:

1. When did you last seriously reflect on the trajectory of your life—where you have been and where you are headed?

2. How does the way you are living now reflect who you really are?

3. What would you like for people to say about you at your funeral?

4. What is The Conversation Project?

5. What hinders you from having an open conversation with your family about end-of-life issues?

6. Review what it means to write an ethical will.

Seven

Defining Beliefs and Their Application to End-of-Life Decisions

People who pray for miracles usually don't get miracles, but people who pray for courage, for strength to bear the unbearable, for grace to remember what they have left behind instead of what they have lost, very often have their prayers answered. —Harold Kushner, author of *When Bad Things Happen to Good People*

IN THE THREE WEEKS after my cardiac arrest, I asked a number of people of various religious and cultural backgrounds why they thought I had survived against the odds. Some people clearly had thought about this question before, others gave a more offhand response.

- Joe (Catholic): "I believe we have folks who look out for us, and sometimes we receive what we sow."

- Moises (nonreligious Jew): "It was a matter of luck. I don't subscribe to the philosophy of Tevye [in *Fiddler on the Roof*] who talked to God and God talked to him and who believed that God was the source of all the good and bad things he experienced."

- Steve (Mennonite): "You are Lazarus, raised from the dead."

- Mark (Catholic): "The stars were aligned just right."

- Muslim doctor: "It's nice you take a positive attitude [of gratefulness] for what happened instead of being bitter."

- Lois (Catholic): "Angels were watching over you."

- Jonas (Amish): "The Lord wasn't finished with you."

- Ivan (Catholic): "With your background as a doctor and your recent [arrest] experience, you have tremendous credibility to bring the science of medicine and spirituality together."

- John (Benedictine monk): "God has something for you to do yet."

- Paul (Orthodox): "Don't spend time trying to figure out why you survived. It is a mystery. Just do what you know to do."

- Mary (Mennonite pastor): "It is good to look for meaning in what happened. We have to accept it as a mystery why some people have favorable outcomes and others do not. It is okay to revel in the good while feeling sad that the outcome was not the same for another person."

- Eldon (hospice chaplain): "You were given the gift of longer life. It is up to you to decide what to do with it."

Some of these responses suggest a predetermined fatalism or just plain luck without any supernatural intervention. Others suggest that God was fully in control and manipulated events according to the divine plan.

FATE, LUCK, OR DIVINE PLAN?

So why did I survive? One possibility is fate—that my future is predetermined and what happens is inevitable, beyond my ability to change. This view says that I have a destiny ordained by an immutable cosmic force that cannot be changed. This is consistent with one person's statement that "the stars were aligned right." Or was it luck—the belief that what happens is purely by chance without any divine intervention or subject to a divine plan? The man driving past a construction site is killed when a crane boom falls, crushing his car. Had he been a half second earlier or later, his life would have been spared. He just had the bad luck to be in the wrong place at the wrong time. Moises, my Jewish friend, would be comfortable with this explanation.

A third possibility is that what happens is all in accordance with a divine plan for me. In execution of the divine plan, God has full control of all things. This explanation gives comfort to many people when a loved one dies. God "needed another angel in heaven" or "it was just his time" that was preordained by God. The corollary to that is that no one dies before their time.

As I thought about these responses to why I survived, several things were clear. As a child, my parents and faith community ingrained into my deepest places of understanding that God exists and God cares. So that's a given for me and not negotiable. But why I survived against the odds remains a mystery. I can't know God's ways and purposes. But having survived, I take to heart the words of Paul from the foregoing responses, "Don't spend time trying to figure out why you survived. It is a mystery. Just do what you know to do," and Eldon, "You were given the gift of longer life. It is up to you to decide what to do with it."

BELIEFS AND PLANNING FOR A GOOD DEATH

The underlying thesis of my book is that everyone deserves a good death. A good death reflects the beliefs and values of the dying person—values like the need to share their dying experience with their family, personal dignity, control over what happens, stewardship of resources, and beliefs about an afterlife. The following pages are designed to address the need for individuals to understand and articulate their values and beliefs that pertain to their time of dying.

> *A good death reflects the beliefs and values of the dying person.*

Defining Beliefs
Exercise 1:

These statements were adapted from the CaringBridge website where people respond to the life-threatening illness of a friend. These statements are from Christians responding to Christians.

Objective: To assist you in articulating what you believe about how God is involved in your life and the lives of others.

Mark "yes" to the statements that you would use in responding to another person in *their time* of uncertainty such as a life-threatening illness. Mark "no" to the statements that you would *not find helpful* if said to you in *your time* of uncertainty. There are no incorrect answers.

If you would like to get a copy of this exercise or any of the ones on the next pages, download them and fill them in without writing in this book. The exercises are available at the MennoMedia store website www.MennoMedia.org/store/LivingThoughtfullyDyingWell.

Yes No

__ __ 1. God gives you strength daily.

__ __ 2. Where is God to allow this to happen?

__ __ 3. We pray that the blood counts will get back to normal.

__ __ 4. We pray you can rest in the knowledge of God's love.

__ __ 5. Let God be in control.

__ __ 6. I lift you up to God for healing and hope.

__ __ 7. Just remember, God is faithful all the time. He loves you more than any of us can.

__ __ 8. God supplies what we need when we need it.

__ __ 9. Keeping you in our thoughts and prayers.

__ __ 10. Jesus is watching over you and will carry you.

__ __ 11. Of course, we are praying for your complete healing!

__ __ 12. I feel God is answering our prayers!!!

__ __ 13. I hope you can feel my love and daily prayers.

__ __ 14. We know who is in control.

__ __ 15. I'm sure there will be some tough times ahead, but God will be with you every step.

__ __ 16. God will have some answering to do (in not answering our prayers).

__ __ 17. I wanted to tell you my mom's story in the hope your "cancer story" may be like hers!

__ __ 18. I am grateful that God is giving you peace.

__ __ 19. During those times of fear and anxiety, I am confident the Spirit will meet you in those places.

__ __ 20. May you feel God's love washing over you, bringing you healing and hope.

__ __ 21. I am also crying—so very, very sad—devastated. I can't imagine how this is for you. I just want to make it all better for you and I can't. Collect my hug and know you are loved.

__ __ 22. I will light a candle for you today, holding you in the light of God's healing love.

__ __ 23. We praise God for skilled physicians, for caregivers who know just what we need, for medicine that makes bodies better, and for the power to survive.

__ __ 24. At adoration this evening, I will hold you in the light.

After you have completed the preceding exercise, I suggest you schedule a time to sit down with your family or church group, using the answers as a basis for discussion. Why did you respond the way you did? How do you experience God's involvement in the details of your daily life? In these discussions, remember that *there are no incorrect answers*. Recognize the vulnerability of each person and hear their comments respectfully and without criticism.

How is God involved in my daily life?
Exercise 2:

Objective: To help you articulate what you believe about how God relates to you.

The table on page 118 asks for a response about how God is involved in the everyday affairs of your life.

Download copies from www.MennoMedia.org/store/ LivingThoughtfullyDyingWell.

In the quiet of your own space or in discussion with others, consider the following three questions. Again, there are no incorrect answers. Respect for one another will allow openness and honesty that builds trust among the participants.

- Does God exist?

- Does God care about me?

- Can and will God intervene for me, even against the laws of nature?

Is there life after this life?
Exercise 3:

Objective: To help you verbalize your beliefs about life after death—the afterlife.

Indicating your agreement or disagreement with the statements on page 119 will help you define what you believe about the existence (or not) of an afterlife.

Download copies from www.MennoMedia.org/store/ LivingThoughtfullyDyingWell.

What I believe about how God is involved in my life

Statement	Strongly agree	Agree	Not sure	Disagree	Strongly disagree
God has a plan for my life and I need to work to fulfill that plan.					
God is in control and I will die only when it is the time for me to die.					
I look to science to provide the ability to heal. I do not pray for miracles.					
God has the power to heal when I turn to God in faith.					
Using the gifts I was born with, it is up to me to make the most of the good and the bad that come my way.					
Nothing in my experience suggests there is a God.					
Why some people survive and others don't in a similar situation is a mystery (not knowable by humans).					
If I am not healed when I pray for healing, it is because I lack faith.					
Because of Jesus, we know that God is with us as we suffer and will bring us to new life before and after death.					
I need to look for the good that may come out of suffering for me and for others.					
God's love is with me through every circumstance, even when I fail.					

What I believe about death and the afterlife

Statement	Strongly agree	Agree	Don't know	Disagree	Strongly disagree
I believe there is life after death.					
I believe that after death we cease to exist in any form.					
I believe that death is a transition to a better place.					
I believe that suffering will end in the afterlife.					
I believe there is a place of suffering and torment in the afterlife.					
I agree with the statement "For me, to live is Christ and to die is gain" (Philippians 1:21).					

How do beliefs about the afterlife affect end-of-life decisions?
Exercise 4:

Objective: To help you define the extent and limits of your end-of-life healthcare.

In the table on page 121, you are asked to identify your desires for end-of-life medical care **taking into account what you believe about how God is involved in your life and the afterlife.**
Download copies from www.MennoMedia.org/store/LivingThoughtfullyDyingWell.

Many persons have found these exercises useful in articulating what they believe, and they have led to meaningful discussions with their family or church-related groups. Families have used these exercises to open conversation across generations that will provide the framework for decisions about end-of-life care. These exercises will prepare you to have the conversation with family members about advance directives where you express your wishes for life-support measures at the end of life.

At some point you will likely be faced with a real-life situation. Then, theories and platitudes no longer suffice. Decisions must be made. See Role-Plays on pages 153-156 for real-life scenarios where end-of-life healthcare decisions are required.

What I want for medical care when I am dying

Statement	Strongly agree	Agree	Don't know	Disagree	Strongly disagree
I want everything done to extend my life, for where there is life there is hope.					
If I am confused, unaware, and unable to relate to others, I don't want life support measures that would extend my life.					
Personal dignity is important to me and I don't want that compromised even though it may shorten my life.					
When further treatment for my condition is considered futile, I want only the care necessary to keep me comfortable.					
I don't want the expenses of my dying to create a financial burden for my family.					
I prefer to die in my own home.					
I prefer to die in a hospital or nursing home.					
If I am dying, I want the consideration of any treatment to include its cost.					

QUESTIONS AND SUGGESTIONS FOR DISCUSSION:

1. As you review the responses in this book as to why the author survived, which statements resonate with you? Which ones don't?

2. What has happened recently in your life or that of others that may push you toward end-of-life planning?

3. Complete Exercises 1 and 2, and then verbalize (in writing or orally to another person) what you believe about the following:

   • Does God exist?

   • Does God care about me?

   • Can and will God intervene for me, even against the laws of nature?

4. Complete Exercise 3. Should your beliefs about how God is involved in your life, and about life after death, influence the extent of life-extending medical measures at the end of life?

5. After completing Exercise 4, try to become comfortable thinking about these issues and then consider discussing your thoughts and feelings with your family, a church group, and your PAHCD.

Eight

Comfort at the Time of Dying through Religious Practices

Before all things and above all things, care must be taken
of the sick, so that they will be served as if they were Christ
in person; for He Himself said, "I was sick, and you visited
Me" (Matthew 25:36), and, "What you did for one of these
least ones, you did for Me" (Matthew 25:40).
—Rule of St. Benedict, Chapter 36

IN THE FOLLOWING PARAGRAPHS, I present the thoughts and actions of four religious practitioners—Catholic, Orthodox, Pentecostal, and Mennonite—as they relate to a dying person. To the casual observer, these sources seem quite disparate in their theology and practice, yet there are many similarities in their practices to bring hope and comfort to the dying. I also include an interview on dying with a compassionate man who considers himself an agnostic.

CATHOLIC (BENEDICTINE MONKS)

The Benedictine monks live by The Rule of St. Benedict written by St. Benedict in the sixth century. Today, in hundreds of monasteries around the world, Benedict's Rule spells out a philosophy of life and instructions to monks in relating to each other in community.

Sixth-century Benedict had no knowledge of CPR, assisted ventilation, tube feedings, kidney dialysis, blood tests, or body scans. Fourteen centuries later, Benedictine abbots continue to apply the Rule despite remarkable changes in lifestyle, social mores, and technology.

When monks get sick, it is the responsibility of the prior to oversee their care. In carrying out these duties, the prior accepts the responsibility to give oversight to the end-of-life care provided to the monks that is consistent with the philosophy of the Rule.

The Rule of St. Benedict says a monk ought to keep death daily in front of his eyes. Their daily thought is that we're pilgrims in this country, that life here has value, but there is more to come. Even though life here is good, there is life still in front of each of us. Monks view this life as a gift and when health fails, try to balance end-of-life expectations with the need to let go. Monks are of the mindset that the transition to the next life will be bigger, better, and more complete.

In the view of the monks, dying can be compared to a ship that leaves the harbor. Everyone watching the departing ship says, "Look! It's getting smaller and smaller." Then it's gone; it's no longer in sight. But the ship is not gone. The problem is our sight, not the ship. If you are on the other side of the ocean, you see the ship arriving. Just as the ship that leaves one side of the ocean and arrives on the other side, so is death a simultaneous leaving and arriving.

Monks see themselves as countercultural in their views of life and death that apply to decisions about their healthcare. As Benedictines, they understand that when it is time to go and God calls, there is no need to delay. "When the bus comes for you, get on the bus. You will know when the bus arrives." The bus arrives for different people at different ages. For example,

Father Kilian at age ninety is still a thoughtful, productive person. On the other hand, some people at age sixty are simply existing and neither thoughtful nor productive.

For a thirty-six-year-old woman who has three children and a young husband, it's understood that all possibilities for treatment will be explored. For monks with their relationship with God and their community, it's not thought to be necessary to do everything that can be done.

The monks have completed advance directives, even thirty-five-year-old monks. One older monk initially said that he wanted everything done to prolong his life. After he saw a video of resuscitation, the nurse explained to him that during CPR, the patient's ribs can be broken and puncture a lung and twenty other bad things can happen. She said that after resuscitation some people survive physically but are in a persistent vegetative state. She said it's nice when you can go quickly, rather than get stuck in dementia. The monk immediately changed his mind and said he didn't want CPR.

Each case is treated differently, based on interaction with the individual. If the monk feels he still has quality of life, the administration will respect the wishes of the individual. For example, Brother Detrick was a younger monk who had brain cancer. He got extensive treatment even though he died as a result of his disease. Another young monk, after he understood the gloomy prognosis of his disease, said, "If this is the way things are going I don't want anything done, so please stop the treatment." In each case, the monks are given the necessary information to make an informed decision.

EASTERN ORTHODOX

Father Matthew Wade described his several-decades-long journey from Evangelicalism to ordination as an Episcopal priest to the Anglo-Catholics. Ten years ago he joined the Eastern Orthodox (Antiochian) Church. His search was propelled by

the observation that confessions were based on personal inter-
pretation of the Scriptures. He was looking for more certainty
and found that in the liturgy of the Eastern Orthodox. He has
been the ordained priest and pastor of an Orthodox church for
five years. In the words of Father Matthew:

> It is important that the priest have an ongoing relationship
> with the parishioner. When a priest walks into a room, he
> embodies the presence and mystery of Christ entering. I try
> to get into all members' homes twice a year. Some people
> just want to talk about their life and their loved ones.
>
> The priest brings the sacrament of the Eucharist. The
> Orthodox faith emphasizes resurrection—resurrection that
> occurs every day, not only on the other side of death. At
> the time of serious illness and terminal illness, the greatest
> thing we can do is to bring the mystery of the presence of
> Christ. People of the Orthodox faith love that. The priest
> draws more closely to the side of that person; specifically,
> the priest brings the Eucharist and offers the bread and the
> wine—the literal body and blood of Christ.
>
> The priest brings the Word, usually from the Psalms or
> from the lectionary. We pray for the soul and body with-
> out separation. We also offer prayer and anointing for
> healing. We pray God's will be done. God's will refers us
> back to baptism. We are baptized into Jesus Christ and
> into his church. It's not what we do; it's what God does for
> us. We constantly say, "God have mercy" and repeat that
> frequently in our liturgy. When we light a candle—and we
> light a lot of candles—we present the desire of the heart as
> we ask God for mercy.
>
> The priest brings the sacrament of confession. Some people
> keep their confession current; others do not and have a strong
> need to free their heart and mind from their transgressions.

The confession is heard by the priest without other family members present. It is a beautiful, beautiful thing to see the release from the burden of their transgressions into the resurrection of Christ. People find great comfort in the sacraments freeing them from fear of impending death.

MENNONITE

Mary Lehman Yoder is an ordained Mennonite pastor and served the same congregation for nearly two decades. She has also served as a hospital chaplain. Mary says:

> As a pastor, it is a great advantage to have a long-term relationship before a person becomes seriously ill. The initial reaction to an acute illness is "I will beat this and return to my normal healthy life." For many people as they get older, they begin to realize that life is getting short. Then there can be a history about how one has lived and how one hopes to die. It is important to make dying a regular and natural part of the conversation.
>
> For some people with a lively view of the afterlife, they see themselves dancing in heaven with their loved ones, restored in body and soul. Some people as death approaches have doubts: "Have I been a good enough disciple of Jesus?" I assure them that they don't *earn* their way into heaven, but it comes from God's love and graciousness. Their entrance into the presence of God is not a reward for their good works but an eternal gift. When a person dies, I don't refer to that as going to their eternal reward.
>
> The Scriptures are helpful, especially Romans 8:39, "[Nothing] will be able to separate us from the love of God," and 1 Corinthians 15, "Behold, I tell you a mystery: We all shall not sleep, but we shall all be changed . . . For this corruptible must put on incorruption, and this mortal must put

on immortality . . . but thanks be to God, who giveth us the victory through our Lord Jesus Christ."[1]

Human touch and open communication are essential. I recall a patient I saw when I was in pastoral education. He was dying of cancer. When we visited him we were dressed like astronauts, including face masks, in order to protect him from harmful infections. His family didn't want him told about his diagnosis or condition because they felt it would take away his hope. In his condition of pain and estrangement from his family, my view was that there was hope in dying. I was able to ask him if there were things he wanted to say to his family and whether there was other unfinished business. The whole process was hampered by not being able to talk openly about the most important thing in the world to him—the fact that he was dying.

There are times when the dying person clearly has hurts, shame, and a need to forgive or be forgiven. Confession and giving these burdens to Jesus can be a time of wonderful release. When that happens, the person's irritating qualities tend to recede or continue to be transformed. When we are at peace within our own spirit, it is a gift not just for our life, but the way we die becomes a gift. This clears the way for a good death that allows for warm remembrances by those that remain.

Myron Augsburger, Mennonite pastor, teacher, and church leader, wrote in response to my question on the Christian source of hope for the dying:

> I have ministered to persons in the last hours of their lives with the words of Jesus, especially from John 14—"Let not your heart be troubled: believe in God, believe also in me. In my Father's house are many mansions; if it were not

---

1. 1 Corinthians 15:51, 53, 57 (ASV).

so, I would have told you; for I go to prepare a place for you. And if I go and prepare a place for you, I come again, and will receive you unto myself; that where I am, there ye may be also."[2]—as well as passages from chapters 15, 16, and 17 with their amazing and wonderful passages of his promise. This is the faith in which we live and die, knowing that our hope is in Him.

AGNOSTIC

Mike Dickson is forty-one years old and has the power of attorney for healthcare decisions for his father, Kirk, who is dying of advanced Parkinsonism. Kirk, as a scientist, is an agnostic with no knowledge or experience to suggest the existence of a supreme or supernatural power. Mike shares those beliefs.

In the words of Mike:

> My father, Kirk, was diagnosed with Parkinsonism a number of years ago. In the last several years his condition gradually deteriorated and he was placed in a nursing home. He remained oriented and responsive until about four months ago. He no longer recognizes or responds to his family.

> Kirk had worked on advance directives. Among those instructions, he asked that if he couldn't eat, he didn't want to be fed. The time came when he was unable to feed himself, yet was able to swallow and appeared to enjoy his food. I and my three brothers came together and decided that he should be fed but reaffirmed Kirk's wishes by agreeing to not allow tube feeding when he could no longer swallow.

> Shortly after admission to the nursing home, Kirk enrolled with hospice. The brothers agree that if he has a cardiac arrest, there will be no CPR. The nurses will call hospice and not EMT.

---

2. John 14:1-3 ASV.

Kirk's views on death and immortality were shaped by his brother Ernest who founded the Church of Religious Science. Ernest said there was more to life than the corporeal and that there was another place after death. We never talked about God in our home. The few times I talked about God, Kirk made it clear very quickly that he didn't want to talk about it. When I asked him if he thought there was this next life, all he would say was, "I think Ernest was right."

Kirk had no sense that good deeds on earth earn one's way to a better place. There is no logical reason why one person would be chosen over another. We exist for a time and we die but something lives on and goes to another place. Where you go is not dependent on religion.

My father's end-of-life decisions are guided purely by what he values, not by religious concerns. If he couldn't live a reasonable life, he wouldn't want to live. A reasonable life to him means to be cognitively functioning—able to communicate and relate. Recently there was only momentary recognition of family members. By all definitions he does not have a reasonable existence here now. The nurses say he used to be a pleasure; he would talk and laugh but now he no longer brings pleasure to anyone. He cannot hold a conversation. He exists only because his body is still functioning. He would not want to be like this. There are no personal beliefs that go into this case, certainly no religious beliefs.

Kirk exists in body only. He was always a logical person and he must have thought about how he can make this [the dying process] work. I am sure that if there were a legal way to hasten the end, he would take it.

PENTECOSTAL

Gary Thomas has been a Pentecostal pastor for seventeen years. At age sixty-four, he is ready to retire. He grew up in a Christian home after his parents' experience of the Holy Ghost completely changed their lives. Gary describes himself during his teenage years as a successful sinner. He was baptized at the age of seventeen when he too received baptism in the Holy Spirit. He felt called to the ministry at age thirty-five and eventually took an extensive home study Bible course and five years later was ordained a Pentecostal pastor.

In the words of Pastor Gary:

My joy in ministry is in giving myself away while helping people through times of trouble. As a pastor relating to people who know they are dying, my foremost concern is that the person is at peace with God and others. Let me tell you about my father's death.

My father was visiting us when at age eighty-seven he developed pneumonia. The doctor told us he probably wouldn't make it. He was struggling for breath and they put an oxygen mask over his face. When he couldn't eat, they inserted a feeding tube. The feeding tube in his nose was clearly uncomfortable, and when he said he wanted the tube removed, the nurse removed it.

Even though my dad was a minister, I asked him, "Are you at peace with God; is there some hidden agenda that you have kept buried in your soul and mind?" He did some soul searching and I heard him say, "God, forgive this old backslidden preacher." That took a lot of guts for someone who was working for God all these years, but showed brutal honesty. I asked him, "Have you settled all of the differences you had with people over all these years?" He assured me it was well with his soul. Then I felt at peace. I saw tears run down the side of my father's face and I know that he was sad leaving his wife and children and grandchildren. Despite that, I thought, "Dad you have done the right thing."

Several days later we transferred him to a nursing home. The doctor told me he wouldn't survive more than twenty-four hours. I again had that talk with him about the state of his soul. He replied, "Son I have lived for this moment all my life." He died later that night.

If I am confronted for the first time with someone who has terminal cancer, I encourage them to do whatever necessary to make peace with God. The first thing my faith says is that God is a healer so I approach God asking for healing. When I ask for healing, I recognize that I can't know God's purposes and ask that God's will be done.

Part of my job is to help people accept the inevitable when further treatment will only prolong their suffering. I recall a person who decided to have back surgery with little chance of success for her incurable cancer. I never saw her when she wasn't moaning in pain. She died so miserably. I have also been at the bedside of people who made different choices, who died in peace. I had talked to them about the place they were going to where there is no pain, no suffering, and there is no sorrow. They died peacefully with that assurance. Personally, the way I feel right now is that if I have a progressive disease such as cancer, I will accept the prognosis and won't seek treatment. This comes from a deep faith in a living Providence.

I find Scripture helpful, especially 1 Corinthians 15:51: "We will not all sleep, but we will all be changed," or passages from Ecclesiastes that say when we pass from this life our bodies go back to dust from whence we came. But the most peaceable part is that our spirit goes back to God. To be absent from the body is to be present with the Lord.

CONCLUSION

Some elements in relating to a dying person were common to all the religious affiliations.

The person dying within a religious framework can be comforted by liturgy, the sacraments, human touch, and loving care. I noticed agreement on the essential elements in ministering to the dying patient among the clergy from disparate religions affiliations. They all affirmed the following expressions of faith and practice:

- The firm belief in an afterlife with death as a transition, not an end

- The need for reconciliation for the dying person with God and other persons

- The importance of providing the dying person the opportunity for confession

- The presence of the clergy bringing comfort to the dying person and family

- The assurance that God is present with them in their time of illness and dying

- The need to bring comfort, peace, and acceptance to the dying person and family

Everyone, whether believer or agnostic, finds hope and comfort in the belief that dying will bring release from their suffering and travail.

QUESTIONS AND SUGGESTIONS FOR DISCUSSION:

1. Discuss with your pastor or priest your thoughts about dying and the afterlife.

2. Consider inviting your pastor/priest to speak to your group about how he or she ministers to a person with a terminal illness.

3. What Scripture or liturgy would you welcome hearing when it is clear you are dying?

4. What is the place for prayers of physical, spiritual, or emotional healing at the end of life?

5. At the end of your life, will you welcome the opportunity for communion, anointing, and confession? Why or why not?

Nine

A Good Death

You take over. I'm about to die, my life an offering on God's altar. This is the only race worth running. I've run hard right to the finish, believed all the way. All that's left now is the shouting—God's applause! Depend on it, he's an honest judge. He'll do right not only by me, but by everyone eager for his coming. —2 Timothy 4:6-8, (*The Message*)

WHEN I DIE

Twenty years ago our family of children and grandchildren, separated by thousands of miles, first gathered for a week of fun and food and games. That first year there were eleven of us, this year, twenty-two. The week is a high priority for everyone and it is rare that anyone misses. Cousins start each week right where they left off twelve months before. Marilyn and I take great delight in seeing our four children and their mates "uncle-ing and aunt-ing" nieces and nephews.

> *I want my time of dying to be a time of strengthening family bonds.*

I want my time of dying to be a time of strengthening these family bonds. So my primary goal in planning for a good death is to preserve and even enhance the relationships among the members of my family. I want to avoid the trap of becoming self-absorbed in my illness; rather, I want to continue to be a caring husband and a loving father and grandfather. I recognize that the *way* I die, not what I die *from,* will either add or detract from the ability of my family to continue to *be* a family.

I am confident that at the time of my dying, my family will provide the physical, emotional, and spiritual comfort for my needs. My confidence is based on the fact that we have discussed limits to my care and the importance of quality of life in considering life-extending measures. My family knows that I don't want my dying process extended, and I don't want to leave a financial burden for my family. In place of frustrations, I hope that my dying will be a time of calmness and even serenity because of the planning that has gone on before.

> *Death can become not an end*
> *but more like a graduation.*

I expect that at the time of my dying, I will be treated with the same dignity accorded to me throughout life. To me, this means that my opinion will be sought if I still have my mental faculties. I recall the time many years earlier when my siblings and I sat at a table discussing my father's future housing and medical needs. My father sat alone on the other side of the large dining room, ignored. I remember that picture with deep regret.

I will not seek to prolong my life when the quality of my life is diminished, for I have seen patients in their last days treated more as an inanimate object and less as a human being. I see no need to squeeze out a few more days or weeks of life when organ systems are failing and I am only intermittently aware of those around me. I hope that my dying will not be seen as a failure of medical science but rather a successful transition to the next life.

If my dying circumstances permit, I want to die at home with the possibility of a proper goodbye to each family member and close friends.

I expect that my dying will be treated as the *spiritual* event that it is. My four months with the Benedictine monks showed me the emphasis the Benedictines place on spirituality as the center of the dying process. In that view, death is a transition from this life to another—not an end, but a continuation. Unlike the medical model that views death as failure, death can become more like a graduation. Like the Benedictines, I want to be able to say goodbye to members of my religious community, and through them to receive the assurance of God's unconditional love and provision for life after this life.

CHECKLIST

I have identified what I need to do to prepare for a good death. I compiled a checklist of tasks and have nearly finished all of them. (See my checklist on page 151.) I can rest in the knowledge that, as much as possible, I created the conditions for my departure that will lighten the load for my family and create good memories.

A GOOD DEATH: VIRGIL'S STORY FROM DENIAL TO HOPE

My brother Virgil, ten years younger than I, had been my closest friend and confidante throughout our adult lives.

Virgil was the picture of health when he was diagnosed with cancer. How could that be? He always took such good care of himself—regular strenuous exercise, eating right, and never overweight. Yet there it was—CANCER.

The instinctive reaction to a crushing medical diagnosis is denial and we look for alternative explanations—the tests are wrong or the doctors missed the diagnosis. After more tests and more discussion with the medical experts, we are forced to accept reality.

Virgil had a highly successful career as CEO of a modest-sized furniture manufacturing plant. Over the years, I listened and learned as his philosophy of leadership in business evolved—what he called servant-leadership. I toured his plants with him and noted how he greeted individual employees by their first name. His wisdom, conciliatory manner, and personal humility propelled him to leadership in many places outside his business, including chairman of the board of Goshen College (Indiana) for ten years. Other business leaders sought his counsel. Over those years, he and Mary Ann became modestly and unpretentiously wealthy. He told me that a number of years ago they decided they had accumulated enough and after that they limited their net worth by increasing their charitable contributions.

At first, all seemed hopeful for Virgil. Doctors were reassuring, and Virgil and Mary Ann heard many stories of men that had lived for years after the diagnosis of prostate cancer. There seemed to be no great urgency to treat the cancer and with the consent of his doctors, he delayed treatment for a month to go on a long-planned family trip to Italy. All the adult members of the family participated in this decision. They agreed that with this and subsequent decisions, there would be no looking back or second-guessing. They wanted no regrets.

LOWERED EXPECTATIONS

The surgery went well and Virg was assured that the cancer was eradicated. However, several months later his biologic marker of prostate cancer—PSA—had reappeared. Hope was still high with assurances that there was medicine to treat the cancer. Gradually they came to understand that while the cancer may be controlled, there would be no cure.

Thereafter there were repeated cycles of hopeful optimism followed by dread and despair as one medicine after another failed. The last high-powered pill appeared to shrink the size of the tumor but the tumor cells mutated to a more virulent and aggressive form and the metastatic tumors spread more rapidly.

At this time, Virg and Mary Ann came to our house prior to going to the cancer clinic. He anticipated that the doctors were going to tell him there was nothing more to offer medically. Now there was no doubt; Virgil's cancer was his terminal disease. Virgil, Mary Ann, Marilyn, and I gathered in a tight circle and wept, crying to God for strength. Hope for a cure was gone and it was clear that his life expectancy would now be measured in weeks or a few months. Virgil was dying.

In addition, Virgil, a self-educated man and nonstop reader, learned that there was no treatment for his progressively failing vision. For Virgil, this news, even more than the cancer, precipitated a severe depression. Even in the depths of his depression, he followed his lifelong pattern of introspection and reflection. His depression cleared after about five weeks. He then went about living his life with all the energy that his cancer allowed, continuing to walk three miles a day until his last hospitalization.

Virgil said on several occasions that he had little tolerance for extensive treatment and that he would come to the point where he would opt for no more treatment. He was clear about his desire for a balance between quality of life and treatment that would induce severe symptoms with little chance of cure. As his cancer progressed, Virgil and his family repeatedly returned to a discussion of his quality of life. As the family discussed these issues, they made it clear that the final decision of when to stop treatment was for Virgil himself to make.

In talking to cancer patients, I repeatedly hear of their need to "adjust to a new normal." As his illness progressed, Virgil was constantly adjusting to new realities and the undeniable signs that the cancer was progressing—loss of appetite and weight, chronic fatigue, increasing pain, and battling the side effects of medicines. These physical signs are a daily reminder of a down-hill course with an end that is impossible to contemplate.

LEANING FORWARD

Virgil's family, who had always been close, began to empha-size even more their times together, snatching times to gather from three states. Virgil and Mary Ann set about get-ting "their affairs in order," which included updating their last will and testament. They went over its provisions with the entire family on a lovely day on the patio.

The family planned carefully for special events, giving careful thought to creating memories for all members of the family, including their four grandchildren. When son-in-law James ran the Boston marathon, all members of the family were on hand to cheer him on, sporting a shirt with a picture of Virgil surrounded by the word *inspiration*.

This is the time for the final preparations for a good death and to ease the path of those remaining. Communication among all family members is essential during this time. The last thing a dying person and his or her family need is mistrust and dissension among family members.

ACCEPTANCE

Later while visiting in Boston, Virg experienced severe pain—in his words: "twenty on a scale of one to ten." Seeing his intense suffering, the family gave him permission to "not fight anymore." It was finally and conclusively apparent to all in the family that any further treatment was futile. Virgil returned to his home in Ohio knowing he had only days to live. He was at peace.

Treatment would no longer be directed to affecting a cure but to keeping him comfortable. They enrolled in hospice with the intention that he would live out his life at home. Virgil appeared utterly at peace.

A GOOD DEATH

Virgil's physical needs were attended to by the family in his own home with help from the hospice nurses. Virgil decided that he would no longer eat and voluntarily stopped all food intake the last three weeks of his life. He did this to decrease the burden on his family and to avoid prolonging the process of dying.

A website devoted to voluntarily stopping eating and drinking (VSED) supports these "legal and peaceful means to end life when physical decline and suffering become pointless and unbearable."[1]

Virgil said he wanted to be home to thank all the people who had been so kind to him. His remaining days were filled with a steady stream of people who came to express their gratitude for his friendship and each in turn heard his affirmation for what they meant to him and how they had touched him. Virgil had the ability to make each person feel that he or she was his special friend. This included all of his thirty nieces and nephews. Each evening his family gathered on or around his bed and together they read the notes of support and encouragement. Virgil died peacefully at home, surrounded by his family.

_____

1. http://www.compassionandchoices.org/tag/vsed/.

Several months after Vigil's death, his son, Brian, said, "I was always impressed by Dad's preparedness. Not just for dying at home, but for dying, period. He had had conversations about his mortality with each of us well before we needed to. This laid the groundwork for a peaceful consent to run through the entire family regarding the last weeks. We'd already said everything that needed to be said, and he had done all that he had needed to do well before then. The 'living out his days' was bonus time. He led us all to be prepared for the eventuality, and he did this well before it was a certainty. Always prepared, always willing to have those hard conversations."

GOOD MEMORIES

The family had lost their major source of encouragement and counsel. Through the pain of separation and loss, they took satisfaction that Virgil's last days were spent as he wanted—in his home and in the company of family and friends. In the weeks after his death, they remembered the times of laughter and tears in the past months and the times of gathering together where there had been no holding back of feelings or expressions of love for each other. Brian also said later, "Insofar as one can accept the final outcome of the death of a beloved father, it could not have been a better experience."

Specific memories will linger indefinitely with the children and grandchildren. As six-week-old granddaughter Sydney and two-year-old Tenley lay on the bed with Virgil, the family noticed the wonderful paradox of the side-by-side new life and approaching death. One evening, when the family gathered in Virgil's bedroom, he said to his two grandsons, Alex and Nickolas, aged fifteen and eleven, "I am sorry I won't be able to see you grow up into the fine men I know you will become." Eleven-year-old Nickolas struck his chest with his fist and said, "Grandpa, you will always be right here in my heart."

Virgil had expressed his expectation that his death would be a transition to another life and that Jesus would see him through. The day before he died, Virgil, although unresponsive, had a broad smile on his face. The family took great comfort in the belief that he had seen something pleasant that beckoned him.

I got the news of Virgil's death at 11:15 p.m. and spent the next several hours remembering Virgil. I recalled the three extended conversations we had over the previous two weeks. The conversations had been without pretense and without any attempt to gloss over the fact that he was dying.

I came away from those talks with fresh insights into what a decent and honorable person Virgil had been. His life was exemplary in many ways, and I felt that he died as he had lived: with nobility of character, with generosity of spirit, and with humility of demeanor. In his last days, he dispensed wisdom and encouragement with quiet sincerity to the many people who visited. He repeatedly offered words of thanks to his visitors for the ways they had enriched and informed his life. He freely expressed his faith that God would accept him in a life after this life. It was apparent that gratitude dominated Virgil's thoughts at the end his life—what a wonderful way to go. What wonderful memories for those of us who remain.

There are helpful lessons to be learned from Virgil's story. In the course of the illness, Virgil and his family

- explored the limits of what medical care had to offer;

- agreed to not second-guess decisions about treatments;

- had open and reality-based conversations about dying;

- considered the quality of life in deciding on the limits of healthcare;

- recognized when further treatment was futile;

- approached death as a spiritual—as well as a physical—event;

- arranged for death to occur at home;

- enlisted the services of hospice;

- intentionally created loving memories that included grandchildren; and

- remembered with gratitude the good life of the past.

MY PLANS FOR MY GOOD DEATH

I have had my conversations with my family and rest assured that they understand my wishes for end-of-life healthcare. I completed my checklist of tasks to be done. A final task remains: to write a letter of requests to my doctor and medical caregivers.

Dear doctor,

I have long faced the fact that my life span is limited. After two myocardial infarctions, quadruple bypass surgery, out-of-sync beating ventricles, an LV ejection fraction of under 35 percent, a heart rhythm dependent on a pacemaker, a cardiac arrest one year ago, and a diagnosis of congestive heart failure, I can no longer deny what's happening. I am dying. It's a reality and I have to deal with it.

As an internist, I have seen both good and bad deaths. My nightmare scenario is to die in an ICU with tubes, catheters, and wires attached, a tube down my throat, my hands tied down, and speech impossible as I struggle for awareness through a haze of illness and sedation. This is not the memory I want the members of my family to carry forward.

When that time comes, when I am remembered rather than present, I want the memories of my death to be as good as those of my life.

In my view, dying is a spiritual as well as a physical event. It shouldn't be approached the way a mechanic approaches repairing a car—find the problem and fix it. I want my death to be a reflection of how I lived that includes the spirituality that has been essential to my being.

I have discussed my wishes for the management of my death with my wife, our son, and our daughter. These discussions took place in a calm atmosphere without the stress of an acute medical crisis. I understand that it's impossible to predict the exact circumstances of my last days. If I am unable to speak for myself when that time comes, I'm confident that the people making decisions for me will do so in the spirit of our discussions. I hope you will honor those discussions as well, viewing my passing not as a failure of modern science but as a transition from one realm to the next.

In deciding what interventions are appropriate, I want my caregivers to consider, above all, my quality of life. If I am suffering from intractable pain or my organ systems are failing, I don't want my life extended by all possible means. I want medical technology to be used only if it will allow me to continue to participate meaningfully in life. When there are several options for further care, include the option of doing less rather than more. Death will come and when it does, I want to die well.

I'm deeply grateful for the advances in medical care during my lifetime. I would not have survived my first heart attack without the improved technology and expertise in treating arrhythmia. And three more times in the last seven years, the application of technological advances saved my life. The fifteen years I gained allowed me to see my children established as contributing members of their communities in healthcare, teaching, and social work. But there is a time to limit technology and let death come.

After what I've been through the past few years, I don't fear death, but I do fear the loss of cognitive ability that would prevent me from relating to others and my surroundings in a meaningful way. As a result, I ask you, as my doctor, to work with my family to honor my wishes. If I have lost my cognitive ability without expectation of return, please turn off my defibrillator. If I am unable to breathe, don't place me on a ventilator. If my heart stops, don't try to restart it. And if I am unable to eat, don't feed me. After a prudent amount of time, if there is no improvement in my condition, turn my pacemaker off.

When I imagine my death, I see myself dying at home, with family and friends able to say proper goodbyes, share in prayers, and leave with comforting rather than disturbing memories. In this scenario, the sadness of separation is tempered by the satisfaction of knowing that their husband, father, grandfather, and friend died well. That he entered the valley of the shadow of death fearing no evil, knowing his God was with him.

Thank you, doctor, in advance, for honoring my wishes.

THE FINAL NOTE

Since my initial heart attack in March 1996, I wake up each morning grateful for one more day of life. The sense of gratitude was reinforced in 2006 when I had coronary bypass surgery and particularly in 2010 at the time of my cardiac arrest. That gratitude propelled me to work daily for a better life for my family and community that would justify my continuing to take up space and use earth's resources.

As I experience decreasing tolerance for physical activity, I know that my heart is less strong than before. I have taken action to prepare the way for my dying time—whether it comes next week or in five years. In doing so, it is my hope that in my last days, I can communicate my love to my family and friends and my deep and humble gratitude for all that life has given me.

When my pacemaker is turned off, the heart monitor will reveal the erratic beat of a too-often injured heart, a heart whose weakness from physical injuries was sublimated to a heart in love with life and made joyful by gratitude for a good life. To the sounds of a final lullaby from family members, the monitor will show the jagged lines of the QRS complex of the heart gradually lengthening to the straight line of a heart that has finally found its rest. I will then enter into the next great adventure that ushers me into the presence of the one who created me.

QUESTIONS AND SUGGESTIONS FOR DISCUSSION:

1. What do you want to be remembered for?

2. Discuss the following: The *way* I die, not what I die *from,* will either add or detract from the ability of my family to continue to *be* a family.

3. As you think about end-of-life medical care, rate the importance of issues like personal dignity and privacy, control over decisions, financial cost, and ready access to your family.

4. Review and discuss the ten things that contributed to making Virgil's death a good death.

5. How did Virgil's family intentionally create loving family memories?

6. How can a family or a church ensure that when a member dies, it is treated more as a spiritual than a physical event?

Epilogue

I CONTINUE TO BE ENGAGED with my family—except for taking a nap whenever they play cards—and with an ever-expanding community. I will resist becoming a bystander as long as I have my strength and my mental faculties.

Throughout my life I was fascinated by the stories of people—stories from farmers in Ohio to farmers in India, the life-changing story of a childhood accident, the story of survival through the holocaust in Cambodia, or the triumph over oppression by a group of Indian women through their collective efforts. I was seldom at a loss for words when meeting a stranger or old acquaintance alike because I always knew there was something to learn from them. I don't recall anyone I considered boring—well, maybe a few after twenty minutes of conversation.

As a young person I recall thinking that when I completed the next phase of life—education or training—I would have things figured out. Then I reached that stage and there was still so much to learn. I discovered that even in my busiest times, it was necessary to find the time to lean back and reflect on what it all means. I came to accept that what I believe to be true today must be open to new learning and understanding. My perceptions and understanding continue to evolve and I will never have it all figured out . . . and when I do, it will be time for me to die.

So even in the ninth decade of life I avidly listen to stories with a view to how it helps me understand life. I take seriously what I hear and test it to see how it adds to or fits with what I believe to be true. In listening to others' stories, I have lost the need to judge; conversely, I am grateful that the other person confides in me.

There are a number of critical decision points in our lives (mine and Marilyn's) where had we taken the other fork in the road, the destination would have been vastly different. In looking back it is not entirely clear how we made those decisions. What is clear is that we were influenced in those decisions by our Anabaptist-Mennonite heritage, a strong sense of community, and the idea that some of our energies needed to be spent in serving others. We tried to take seriously the words of Jesus on how to live and relate. We preferred hospitality and gentleness to coercion and confrontation. The thread that seems to run though our varied experiences is the desire to serve. In serving we were in turn served by so many along the way. For that, I am grateful.

The words of Indian Nobel Prize winner Rabindranath Tagore ring true:

> I slept and dreamt that life was joy.
> I awoke and saw that life was service.
> I acted and behold, service was joy.

Checklist

I REPEAT ONCE MORE: a good death doesn't just happen—it takes planning and the completion of specific tasks. Following is my checklist:

✓ 1. Last will and testament updated with a named executor

✓ 2. Meeting with my executor for

- Access to financial records, both printed and computer files
- User IDs and passwords
- Lists of regular payments and sources of income
- Social security changes after my death
- Instructions for stopping supplemental insurance and long-term care payments

✓ 3. Living will and advance directives prepared

- Have "the conversation" with family members about end-of-life preferences (see page 152 reference to the website http://theconversationproject.org/ to prepare for "the conversation" with your family)
- Power of attorney for healthcare decisions (PAHCD) identified
- Advance directives discussed in detail with PAHCD and other family members
- Advance directives filed with
  - PAHCD
  - Hospital
  - Doctor(s)
  - Pastor
  - Attorney
  - Check with EMT if DNR is in place

✓ 4. Tidy up frayed personal relationships
   - Clear old sources of conflict or misunderstandings
   - Words of affirmation to family and friends
   - Thanks to persons who contributed to me over my lifetime
   - Cultivate a sense of gratitude for a life well lived
   - Discuss with family or others unfinished projects

✓ 5. Psychological/spiritual preparation
   - Family discussions
   - Group for prayer and psychological support

✓ 6. Pass on specific items and mementos to family members and friends

✓ 7. Funeral plans and preferences
   - Meet with funeral director
   - Communicate with clergy, children, and executor
   - Write an obituary

✓ 8. Prepare a list of people to notify about my death
   - Friends and family
   - Agencies such as Social Security and other financial agencies

✓ 9. Write an ethical will for my children and grandchildren (see page 71)

✓ 10. Write a letter to my doctor that summarizes my wishes for end-of-life care

QUESTIONS AND SUGGESTIONS FOR DISCUSSION:

1. Which task(s) on the checklist is unclear?

2. Which task will you find most difficult?

3. Check the website http://theconversationproject.org/ to prepare for "the conversation" with your family.

Role-Play

REAL-LIFE MEDICAL DILEMMAS

Following are real-life clinical situations that call for a decision. Many of these examples represent dilemmas with no easy answers. Put yourself in the role of the decision maker. I encourage you to struggle with these situations and assure you that it will serve you well when this or a similar circumstance arises. You may want to discuss these in a church or family group.

Several questions can guide your thinking:

- Are there advance directives that inform this decision?

- Apart from AD, has the patient expressed his or her preferences in this or a similar situation?

- What course of treatment is most consistent with the patient's theology, including views of the afterlife?

- Are there values of the patient that need to be respected, such as privacy, dignity, control, and cost?

- Is there a moral line being crossed with one decision over another?

1. A woman, age sixty-five, has metastatic lung cancer. No more treatment is available for the cancer. She is bedridden and suffering, requiring increasing pain medication. She now develops pneumonia. She has no advance directives. The doctor needs to know how much and what kind of treatment is desired in this situation. She is delirious and unable to make decisions. If this is your mother: Do you want hospitalization, antibiotics, assisted ventilation, tube feeding, and resuscitation if necessary? What would you want if you were the patient?

2. Your father, age sixty-nine, with Alzheimer's disease, is now confused and does not recognize his family members. On admission to a nursing home you are asked about a DNR (do not resuscitate) order. The patient had never expressed himself on this issue with his family. You are one of three children. How do you decide? What would you advise?

3. What if the man with Alzheimer's disease just isn't as mentally sharp as before? He has poor short-term memory but is otherwise in good health and is still living at home and relates to his family. Should he have a DNR order?

4. Imagine you are an eighty-seven-year-old man, alert and moderately active. You consult a surgeon for a non-painful lump in the groin that turns out to be a hernia. The surgeon offers to repair the hernia. The risk of surgery is low. What questions do you ask in order to make your decision?

5. You choose to have the surgery. It is noted that you have a slow heart rate and a pacemaker is advised before the surgery. Cost: $40,000. Medicare will pay most of the cost of the pacemaker. Do you still go ahead with the surgery?

6. A fifty-six-year-old woman has breast cancer that is no longer curable. The doctor says there is a 50 percent chance that the drug Avastin will increase survival by six to twelve weeks. The side effects of the drug include loss of appetite, nausea, and occasional vomiting. The drug cost is $55,000 per year (about $4,500 per month). What do you do if insurance covers the cost? If insurance *does not* cover the cost?

7. An eighty-year-old man with congestive heart failure tolerates only minimal activity because of shortness of breath and leg swelling. The cardiologist advises revamping the pacemaker with a surgical procedure that 50 percent of the time will improve the heart efficiency and exercise tolerance by 15 percent. Estimated cost: $45,000. There is no

guarantee that it will prolong life. Do you agree to the procedure to change the pacemaker?

8. After suffering a stroke, an eighty-four-year-old man is unable to talk, bedridden, and intermittently confused. Five years earlier he asked that his pacemaker would be turned off if he has lost his cognitive ability. If you are the PAHCD, will you ask the cardiologist to do that?[1]

9. A man, eighty-nine, has a tumor in his pancreas that is "probably benign but may not be." His surgeon offers to follow the tumor every three months to see if it is growing or to surgically remove it now. What questions do you have? How will you choose?[2]

10. You are the PAHCD for your mother, seventy-four, in the end stages of metastatic colon cancer. She has lost considerable weight and requires increasing amounts of pain medicine. She is unable to eat or take fluids. The only way to give fluid and nutrition is by IV line. This issue was never discussed with her. Do you agree to give her IV fluids?

11. Your husband (eighty-seven) of many years is getting increasingly frail. He states he is ready to die and wants no life-extending measures. One morning he wakes up with weakness on his left side—obviously a stroke. He is alert. What do you do: Call EMT? Go to the hospital? Submit to invasive tests? Agree to surgery if advised?

12. Your mother, at age ninety-two, has been in a nursing home for four years. She has been confused and hasn't recognized you on your weekly visits for two years. She now gets pneumonia. The nursing home calls you, her PAHCD, to report

---

1. Crystal Phend, "Cardiac Device Deactivation Not Euthanasia, Society Says," *MedPage Today*, May 14, 2010, http://www.medpagetoday.com/MeetingCoverage/HRS/20119.

2. Paula Span, "Who Thrives after Surgery?" *New York Times*, December 28, 2010, http://newoldage.blogs.nytimes.com/2010/12/28/who-thrives-after-surgery/.

that the doctor wants her in the hospital. Do you have the right to request that she not be hospitalized? What questions will help you make a decision?

The above scenarios are not theoretical but based on actual situations in my medical practice. Even though it is hard, I encourage you to wrestle with the above examples. It will be of great benefit to have discussed these issues well before a medical crisis when emotions run high and there is urgent need for decisions.

QUESTIONS AND SUGGESTIONS FOR DISCUSSION:

1. These scenarios are excellent to discuss with a church group, family, and your PAHCD.

2. If you are over sixty-five or have a terminal illness, imagine yourself as the patient discussing with your family and PAHCD your feelings and preferences even though this does not fit your situation perfectly.

3. If you are a PACHD for a family member, find ways to discuss these scenarios with that person. This discussion can be part of "the conversation."

Appendix 1

ABBREVIATIONS AND DEFINITIONS

AD: advance directives; a listing of preferences and limitations for medical care at the end of life; called ACP—Advance Care Plan—in Canada

ALS: amyotrophic lateral sclerosis; a degenerative nerve disease without effective treatment or cure; often referred to as Lou Gehrig's disease

antisepsis: sterilization or destruction of microorganisms that cause disease

BUN: blood urea nitrogen; a major measurement of kidney function

CaringBridge: a website where people or families with a serious health problem can share updates and receive support from others (CaringBridge.org)

CHF: congestive heart failure; a condition of fluid accumulation and decreased tolerance for physical activity due to a weakened heart, usually progressive

COPD: chronic obstructive pulmonary disease

CPR: cardiopulmonary resuscitation; the attempt to reestablish a functional heart rhythm in the event of ventricular fibrillation (see below) or to reestablish ventilation at a time of respiratory arrest

CT: computed tomography; a noninvasive scanning technique; also called a CAT scan (computer axial tomography)

DNR: do not resuscitate; a request from a patient that in the event of a cardiac arrest, there will be no efforts to resuscitate

defibrillator: a device that emits an electric charge that shocks the fibrillating heart back into an effective rhythm

EKG: electrocardiogram; a recording of the electrical activity of the heart

EMT: emergency medical technician; a person trained to give emergency medical care

ER: emergency room

heart catheterization: a procedure where a small tube (catheter) is passed through a vein into the heart with the insertion of dye to outline the anatomy of the heart and its arteries; this procedure is necessary before a stent is placed and before open heart surgery

ICD: implantable cardiac defibrillator; the small device placed under the skin in the upper chest that can shock the heart to reestablish an effective rhythm after the onset of ventricular fibrillation

ICU: intensive care unit

IV: intravenous; fluid or medicines given directly into a vein

LV: shorthand for left ventricle or left ventricular, the largest chamber of the heart

LW: living will; a document from a patient that instructs medical caretakers regarding the patient's wishes on limitations for life-extending measures

MRI: magnetic resonance imager; a noninvasive scanning technique that provides detailed images of internal body structures

PAHCD: power of attorney for health care decisions; a surrogate who speaks for the patient who cannot speak for him/herself to make necessary healthcare decisions

PET: positron emission tomography; a scan taken after the injection of a radioactive tagged glucose-like substance; areas of inflammation or cancer burn up the glucone faster with a concentration of the radioactivity recorded by the scan, thereby locating and estimating the size of any cancer present

PTSD: post-traumatic stress disorder; a mental illness caused by a traumatic event and characterized by reliving the event with attendant distressing emotions and physical symptoms

QRS complex: the combination of the three deflections of the electrical activity of the heart recorded by the electrocardiogram (EKG)

ventricular fibrillation: the chaotic uncoordinated electrical activity of the largest chamber of the heart and the usual cause of cardiac arrest (note: *atrial fibrillation* affects the upper chambers of the heart and in itself is not a cause of cardiac arrest)

Appendix 2

Comparison of U.S. and Canadian Systems of Healthcare[1]		
	United States	Canada
Percent who support universal healthcare (poll 2003)	62%[1]	90%
Percent who have access to healthcare (insured)	Approx. 85% (2013)	Approx. 100%
Percent who are satisfied or very satisfied (2011)[2]	25%	57%
Percent who wait more than four weeks for a specialist appointment (2010)[3]	20%	59%
Life expectancy[4]	78.7 years	80.9 years
Infant mortality (deaths/1000 live births)[5]	6.8	5.2
Source of financing	60% government, Medicare/Medicaid, Military/veterans/government employees 20% business through insurance 20% out of pocket	70% publically financed single payer system 30% private insurance with 2/3 paid by employers
Administrative costs (percent of total costs)[6]	31%	16.7%
Percent of GDP for healthcare[7]	17.4%	11.4%
Per capita cost per year (USD) (2009)[8]	$8,223	$4,445

1. Sources for chart on page 160: Except for footnoted items, all of the information in the above table was extracted from "Comparison of the health care systems in Canada and the United States." This is an extensive and authoritative treatment of the subject that cites 159 references. http://en.wikipedia.org/wiki/Comparison_of_the_health_care_systems_in_Canada_and_the_United_States (accessed August 28, 2013).

2. Gary Langer, "Health Care Pains: Growing Health Care Concerns Fuel Cautious Support for Change," (Poll conducted October 9–13, 2003) ABC News/*Washington Post*, October 20, 2003, http://abcnews.go.com/sections/living/US/healthcare031020_poll.html.

3. Sarah Kliff, "Everything You Ever Wanted to Know about Canadian Health Care in One Post," *Washington Post*, July 1, 2012, http://www.washingtonpost.com/blogs/wonkblog/wp/2012/07/01/everything-you-ever-wanted-to-know-about-canadian-health-care-in-one-post/.

4. Ibid.

5. Ibid.

6. "List of Countries by Infant Mortality Rate," Wikipedia, http://en.wikipedia.org/wiki/List_of_countries_by_infant_mortality_rate (figures are from the 2011 United Nations World Population Report and 2013 CIA World Factbook).

7. Steffie Woolhandler, MD, MPH et al., "Costs of Health Care Administration in the United States and Canada," New England Journal of Medicine 349 (August 21, 2003): 768–75, http://www.nejm.org/doi/pdf/10.1056/NEJMsa022033.

8. See Sarah Kliff, note 3, above.

Appendix 3

RESOURCES

1. Advance directives or advance care plan

   a. U.S. Living Will Registry: "Protect your right to control your health care. Learn how to create and register your living will and health care proxy." http://www.uslivingwillregistry.com/

   b. Advance Care Planning in Canada: National Framework. http://www.advancecareplanning.ca/media/40158/acp%20framework%202012%20eng.pdf

   c. (Canada) Speak Up: "It's about conversations. It's about decisions. It's how we care for each other." http://www.advancecareplanning.ca/

   d. Physician Orders for Life-Sustaining Treatment (POLST). http://www.cdph.ca.gov/programs/LnC/Documents/MDS30-ApprovedPOLSTForm.pdf

   e. Compassion and Choices. http://www.compassionandchoices.org/what-we-do/advance-planning/advance-directive/

2. Ethical will

   a. Barry K. Baines, *Ethical Wills: Putting Your Values on Paper,* (Cambridge, MA:Da Capo Press, April 20, 2009, 2nd edition).

   b. Celebrations of Life, Ethical Wills/Legacy Letters. http://celebrationsoflife.net/ethicalwills/

3. Prepare to talk to your doctor

   a. WebMD: Pose a question and receive an easy-to-read answer. www.webmd.com

b. *The Merck Manual Home Health Book for Patients and Caregivers.* http://www.merckmanuals.com/homeindex. html

c. Agency for Healthcare, Research and Quality: "Questions to ask your doctor." http://www.ahrq.gov/patients-consumers/patient-involvement/ask-your-doctor/index.html

4. Books and articles

a. Ira Byock, MD, *The Best Care Possible: A Physician's Quest to Transform Care through the End of Life* (New York: Penguin Books, 2009).

b. Ira Byock, MD, *Dying Well: Peace and Possibilities at the End of Life* (New York: Riverhead Books, 1997).

c. Maggie Callanan and Patricia Kelley, *Final Gifts: Understanding the Special Awareness, Needs, and Communications of the Dying* (New York: Simon & Schuster, 2012).

d. Peter Fenwick and Elizabeth Fenwick, *The Art of Dying* (New York: Continuum, 2008). A contemporary version of the medieval *Ars Moriendi*, a manual on how to achieve a good death.

e. David Kessler, *The Needs of the Dying: A Guide for Bringing Hope, Comfort, and Love to Life's Final Chapter* (New York: HarperCollins, 2007) (10th anniversary edition).

f. Rob Moll, *The Art of Dying: Living Fully into the Life to Come* (Downers Grove, IL: InterVarsity Press, 2010).

g. Glen E. Miller, *Empowering the Patient: How to Reduce the Cost of Healthcare and Improve Its Quality* (Indianapolis, IN: Dog Ear Press, 2009).

h. Suleika Jaoud, "Life Interrupted: Six Ways to Live with Cancer," *New York Times,* August 23, 2012, http://well. blogs.nytimes.com/2012/08/23/life-interrupted-six-ways-to-cope-with-cancer/?ref=health. Written by a twenty-four-year-old woman with leukemia who outlines ways to live with the uncertainty of cancer.

i. Paula Span, *When the Time Comes: Families with Aging Parents Share Their Struggles and Solutions* [Kindle Edition], (New York: Springboard Press, 2009).

Video/DVD

Embracing Aging: Families Facing Change, Mennonite Media, 2007. Features Dr. Ira Byock, Lynn Miller, and others on preparing yourself and family for the "third stage" of life: housing, illness, caring for aging parents. 58 minutes.

Topical Index

The Author

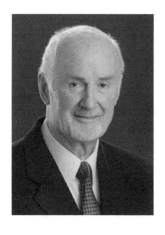

Born on a farm in northwest Ohio, Glen Miller's vocation and motivations took him to more than forty-four countries. Lacking any outside financial help, he worked his way through undergraduate and medical school. His abilities were recognized early in his career as he accepted leadership roles on the medical staff and in hospital administration, eventually as medical director. Over twenty-five years, he played a key role in elevating the local hospital in Bellefontaine, Ohio, to the top rung of small hospitals in the state. Along the way his commitment to life-long learning led to training and certification in internal medicine and a masters in theological studies.

After graduation from medical school and internship, Dr. Miller went with his young family to serve the medical needs of the poor in Haiti. This helped shape his worldview with an awareness of the vast unmet needs in developing countries. In response, he spent eleven years in medical care, teaching, and development activities with Mennonite Central Committee in Haiti, Egypt, India, and Cambodia. Along the way he found encouragement and inspiration from many people like Mother Teresa in Calcutta.

Dr. Miller is retired and lives in Goshen, Indiana, with his wife, Marilyn, and is fully involved in the activities of Assembly Mennonite Church. His four children and their spouses are engaged in education, healthcare, or social work. He follows with close interest the growth and maturation of his grand-children. Dr. Miller is the author of *Empowering the Patient: How to Reduce the Cost of Healthcare and Improve Its Quality* (Indianapolis, IN: Dog Ear Publishing, 2009).